P9-AOY-131

Succession

Succession

The Political Reshaping of British Columbia

David J. Mitchell

Douglas & McIntyre
Vancouver/Toronto

To my mother

Douglas & McIntyre Ltd., 1615 Venables Street, Vancouver, British Columbia   V5L 2H1

Canadian Cataloguing in Publication Data

Mitchell, David Joseph.
　Succession

　　Includes bibliographical references and index.
　　ISBN 0-88894-566-3

　　1. British Columbia — Politics and government — 1975- 2. British Columbia Social Credit Party.
　I. Title.
　FC3828.2.M58 1987　　　320.9711　　　C87-091160-0

Design by Barbara Hodgson
Typeset by The Typeworks

Printed and bound in Canada by Imprimerie Gagné Ltée

The excerpt from the column by Marjorie Nichols is used by permission of the Vancouver Sun.

Contents

Acknowledgements

Succession was researched and written during the twelve months following the Social Credit leadership convention at Whistler, B.C., 28–30 July 1986. The many persons to whom I am indebted are far too numerous to mention by name, but I express my thanks to all of those who shared with me their opinions, arguments and reflections on the subjects covered by this book.

I would like to acknowledge a special debt of gratitude to all those who were brave enough to allow me to tape record their comments and observations so that I could use their voices to help describe the events, issues and personalities of British Columbia's recent past. In particular former premier, Bill Bennett, and the current premier, Bill Vander Zalm, were accessible and co-operative, and I thank both of them for their time, patience and candour.

The many intrepid members of British Columbia's news media who assisted me directly and indirectly must also be recognized. Through their work, the fourth estate has become an integral —although not always responsible—part of British Columbia's political culture. I would like to especially note the assistance and friendship of Vaughn Palmer, surely the hardest working political columnist in Canada's Pacific province.

I would be negligent if I did not thank Sandy Fulton for bearing with me when my labours on this book might have made me unbearable.

Finally, I must acknowledge the support of my family. My wife, Marlene, with patience and without exasperation typed and retyped the manuscript—thereby reading a book which otherwise might not have made it onto her reading list. And my daughters, Madeleine and Jane, have made my life terribly convenient, learning to live and learn and grow both with and without me.

Preface

The recent transition of power on Canada's west coast dramatically shows how a change in leadership can rejuvenate and redirect a political party, a government and a province. It also demonstrates some of the universal traits which accompany the onerous responsibilities and tremendous pressures of political leadership in a modern democratic society.

To change leaders of a governing political party without losing power will forever be a delicate and daunting task. In British Columbia this is especially true. The province's political culture is not static; it is a constantly changing, dynamic culture. The only continuity is provided by the politics of personality that gives populist leaders inordinate power in shaping the province's future. In a polarized culture such as British Columbia's, leadership becomes the crucial factor in any political equation. It is probable, and perhaps even desirable, that where a country or a province is divided between two blocs, each of them will and should some day come to power. However, the recent succession of leadership in British Columbia's governing party has prevented this from happening and has also made the Social Credit Party the unlikely model of political succession in Canada.

In large part this was all made possible by Bill Bennett and his brilliant, unexpected and sad departure from public life. It is espe-

cially timely to review the premiership and the legacies of the
enigmatic Bennett, the politician who was unafraid to launch the
restraint revolution in Canada, who managed the provincial government during the throes of the worst economic recession in half a
century and who left politics undefeated and unloved.

"We fight for lost causes because we know that our defeat and
dismay may be the preface to our successors' victory, though that
victory itself will be temporary," wrote T. S. Eliot. Bennett could
plan the timing and many of the details of his succession, but he
could not choose his successor. Yet it would be left up to his replacement to prove the dream of institutionalizing the Social
Credit Party beyond the leadership of the Bennetts of Kelowna.
Also resting on his successor's shoulders would be the weight of
determining whether or not British Columbia's public sector
restraint program was simply an aberration—a temporary interruption in the collectivist trend of the twentieth century—or a sustainable effort to radically reduce the size and scope of government.

When it comes to the important political issues of style and technique, Bill Bennett and his successor, Bill Vander Zalm, are a
study in contrasts. If Vander Zalm and Bennett are seen to be playing a good cop/bad cop routine, it was certainly not planned that
way. But Bennett left the government and his party in a good
enough condition that any successor would be well positioned to
capitalize on an overwhelming desire for change. Bennett took the
poison with him when he retired from the scene. And the remarkable fact is that he did so willingly.

Bill Vander Zalm now has the rare opportunity to lead, to develop his own vision for a reindustrialization of British Columbia
and to leave a permanent imprint on his province. The apparent
differences between his government and the one led by Bill Bennett are so great that the Bennett era is already almost forgotten.
Over time, however, Bill Bennett's record as a politician and government leader must be remembered; his achievements should be
recognized; his mistakes should not be repeated.

As British Columbia makes the voyage from Bill Bennett to Bill
Vander Zalm, and its governing party—the Bennett party
—becomes the Vander Zalm party, the new leader faces a self-
imposed challenge of reshaping the politics of his province. The
proof of Vander Zalm's leadership will be in the building up of the
expertise, the talent—the team—within his party and within his

government that will help him fulful his vision. There can be little doubt that Premier Vander Zalm has the ability to be a great leader in the populist tradition of west coast politics. And, like all leaders, he has the opportunity to defeat himself. As W. A. C. Bennett once warned: "Governments are defeated from within."

In every picture there must be shade as well as light. If we can now begin to judge Bennett, it is too early to provide any detailed commentary or critique of Bill Vander Zalm as a leader. To rush in on him before his significance has had time to separate from current circumstances can be dangerous. Surely it is audacious even to attempt to chronicle history while it is still smoking. Nonetheless, the story so far is well worth telling. Truth is more interesting, if sometimes less believable, than fiction.

CHAPTER 1

Winners and Losers

"You and I can both live in the same town and run successful businesses. We can both be lawyers and do well. We can both be doctors and have successful practices. But we can't both be successful politicians. In politics, only one can succeed."

These are the sage words of W. A. C. Bennett, the longest-serving premier in the history of British Columbia and a seminal force in the province's development. Politics, in British Columbia as everywhere, is about winners and losers. In no other field of human endeavour—save perhaps professional sports—are performance and personal worth measured so severely. Losers are quickly forgotten. Winners describe and explain the past, they illuminate the present and they help shape the future. W. A. C. Bennett was a winner.

To understand British Columbia and its politics, W. A. C. Bennett and his achievements must be understood, for his legacies continue to play an important part in the province. For an entire generation, he *was* politics; he ruled supreme in Victoria from 1952 to 1972, winning seven consecutive general elections at the helm of the Social Credit Party of B.C. During a period of the greatest economic expansion in Western industrial history, the consistency of W. A. C.'s vision and the strength of his leadership significantly shaped the rise of British Columbia.

The memory of Wacky—as he was known by friend and foe alike—conjures images of a simpler time when British Columbians revelled in the Good Life, when Canada's Lotus Land was a prosperous, magical corner of the world.

Life in British Columbia, however, was never really that easy. And neither was W. A. C. Bennett always a winner. The self-made hardware merchant from the Okanagan entered provincial politics in 1941, after an unsuccessful attempt at a Tory nomination in 1937. He served for almost three full terms as a backbench MLA in the Liberal-Conservative coalition, during which time he worked away at his ambitions and frustrations in a long series of personal defeats. W. A. C. never received a coveted cabinet post, he was twice defeated in his bid for the leadership of the B.C. Conservative Party, and he even lost a 1948 federal by-election. By the time he reached his early fifties, the well-worn W. A. C. had a catalogue of humiliating defeats to his name. Still he persevered.

In 1951 he bolted from his party and sat as an independent MLA. He considered forming a new political party, but then joined the fledgling Social Credit movement. Few British Columbians at the time had ever heard of Social Credit; those who had considered it a ragtag collection of kooks and cranks. But W. A. C. discerned in this group both the organizational basis for a new political force as well as his own main chance. Within six months of joining Social Credit, which had never before elected a single member in the province, W. A. C. Bennett was the premier of British Columbia. From this bold gamble, he did not look back.

Clearly this is the stuff of legends. W. A. C. had lost many battles along his personal path to power, but he learned to trust his intuition. He acquired an almost unerring ability to know when to go forward and when to duck; "Timing is everything," he was fond of saying. His political triumphs often seemed like single, bold strokes and may have been based upon hunches, but they were also part of a long, slow fermentation process. His practise of the art of politics—which he liked to call a science—was the distillation of years of training and experience. Combined with his independence, high moral standards and an uncanny ability to accurately read the mood of the public on most major issues, W. A. C. Bennett emerged as a formidable populist leader.

In British Columbia, Social Credit is best understood as an indigenous movement of protest against established political elites.

Socialists and other political opponents of Social Credit in British Columbia mistakenly assumed that this new force was an extension of the Liberal-Conservative coalition that had governed the province throughout the 1940s. This profound misunderstanding helped sustain Social Credit in power.

Although the movement had featured both religious fundamentalists and monetary fetishists in its early years, when W. A. C. Bennett adopted Social Credit and rode it as his vehicle to power in 1952 its basic nature was transformed. The name remained, but the goals and policies of Social Credit evolved to reflect the personality of its leader and his well-considered views about the development of British Columbia. As such, Social Credit emerged as a strident political force in British Columbia—an independent, conservative, populist party with a strong base of support in the interior hinterland. Social Credit was the W. A. C. Bennett Party.

The many critics who suggested that W. A. C. was a one-man government were correct. During his two decades as premier, his leadership style was highly centralized, and for most of that period he also held the finance portfolio, thereby strengthening his grip over all departments and agencies of the provincial government. Even during the late 1960s and early 1970s, as west coast society became more complex and fragmented and demands on government grew rapidly, W. A. C. continued to run his own show single-handedly. Ministers in his cabinet never had any doubt who was in charge.

W. A. C.'s leadership style was uncluttered. A sign hanging in his office in the parliament buildings carried the motto "K. I. S. S."—Keep It Simple, Stupid. Neither he nor his ministers maintained any of the trappings of government so common today. Cabinet met regularly, but with no officials present and no formal minutes or record of decisions, save for the orders-in-council that were approved. There were no executive or ministerial assistants, press secretariats or policy advisers.

The focus for ministers was kept strictly on the operation of their departments. The development, formulation and co-ordination of policy was a responsibility of neither the public service nor of cabinet, but rather of the premier himself. W. A. C. Bennett believed that devising policy was the proper role and responsibility of a leader.

The myriad policy initiatives that emanated from Victoria during

W. A. C.'s years were invariably bold, aggressive and controversial. During that period of unprecedented economic expansion, British Columbia's resources and products were much in demand. W. A. C. Bennett, riding this rolling wave of prosperity and burgeoning government revenues, opened up the interior of the province with new roads, highways and bridges, constructed massive hydroelectric generating dams and built the infrastructure for further economic development—appropriate undertakings, he believed, for a government in a resource-rich frontier.

In an era before the word *privatization* was known, W. A. C.'s government nationalized or "provincialized" the B.C. Electric Company, creating a giant crown corporation, B.C. Hydro. The government also purchased a ferry fleet and conceived the B.C. Ferry Corporation, built and expanded the provincially owned British Columbia Railway, and even attempted to create, with public funds, a provincial bank. (A scaled-down, privately owned version of the premier's vision, the Bank of British Columbia, started business in 1966.) For W. A. C. Bennett, crown-owned enterprises served both as aggressive agents of provincial development and as shining examples of the kinds of services a well-managed government could provide.

W. A. C. Bennett's stewardship of the B.C. economy was consistent with trends across Canada and throughout the Western world. Year by year, as the role of governments in the economy has increased, the share of the private sector has declined. W. A. C.'s view was that government should provide the basic services upon which productive, wealth-generating activities could grow and thrive. Yet more than any other B.C. premier in modern times, he encouraged British Columbians to rely upon the provincial government to promote their well-being. Although he advocated an economic system based upon free enterprise and private initiative, in truth he was a practising interventionist.

W. A. C. also promoted the idea of ever-increasing material wealth. The problem with his visionary outlook was that, once raised, economic expectations are not easily lowered. His economic achievement—the rapid rise and industrialization of British Columbia during the 1950s and 1960s—was a tough act for later governments to follow.

One of W. A. C. Bennett's political legacies was the polarization of B.C. politics. British Columbia is the only province where neither of the two traditional national parties play a provincial role. The Social Credit Party and the New Democratic Party are the two alternatives. W. A. C. Bennett deliberately promoted this two-party system to prevent a resurgence of the Grits and Tories. He established Social Credit as the province's only private enterprise party, the alternative to socialism.

From time to time British Columbians have flirted with the idea of reviving one of the old-time parties or of developing a "third force" in B.C. politics, but to be a provincial Liberal or Conservative since Bennett's time has been to engage in quixotic adventurism on the lunatic fringe. Although it sustained him in power for twenty years, W. A. C.'s political achievement was flawed, and the flaw ensured his eventual defeat. For in a democratic two-party system it is likely, and probably desirable, that the alternative party will be given a chance to govern. Unless of course the governing party can manage the delicate task of regenerating itself and arranging for succession of leadership without losing the reins of power.

Hand-in-hand with polarization came the paranoid style of B.C. politics: good guys versus bad guys; fear and loathing; class conflict. The paranoid style suggests an urgent need to make the right decision and cast the right vote lest the future of the province and the livelihood of its workers and their children be ruined—perhaps for all time. Social Credit came to power in British Columbia at the same time that McCarthyism and red-baiting were at a peak in the United States. W. A. C. Bennett perfected a local version of the paranoid political style when he predicted the disastrous results of a socialist victory in the province. "The socialist hordes are at the gates!" he would exclaim during election campaigns. His style was easily adopted by the NDP, when they preached about the evils of capitalism and the exploitation of B.C. workers by the captains of industry. All in all it produced much wild rhetoric, an exaggerated emphasis on political ideology, and "true believers" on both sides of the political spectrum.

Populism is another strong theme in B.C. politics that emerged and took hold during W. A. C. Bennett's years in office. Under his leadership, Social Credit's image was as an anti-establishment party, and W. A. C. did his utmost to develop a track record for representing the concerns of ordinary citizens rather than established forces or moneyed interests. He fought to represent *all* British Columbians—the "little people," as he called them. He carefully cultivated the image of the battling outsider, the man who spoke not for one group or class but, with a certain deep conviction and heavy emphasis, for *the people*. This has produced in British Columbia a tradition of distrust towards large, powerful organizations such as big business, organized labour and the federal government in far-off Ottawa. In the operation of provincial government it has meant a unique and at times impractical emphasis on elected representatives, rather than nonelected officials, being in charge.

Fiscal credibility is another of W. A. C. Bennett's political legacies. As premier and minister of finance he ran a tight ship and encouraged British Columbians to regard his government as the miracle mechanic of the economic machine and to look at him as a wily old financial wizard working wonders on behalf of the people. Each and every year he spent more and borrowed more and yet boasted of a debt-free province with forever-balanced budgets. Indeed, balanced budgets became a Social Credit trademark, and deficit spending a bugbear. This tradition of fiscal credibility and balanced budgets became so firmly entrenched that governments facing the extremely volatile economic conditions of the 1970s and '80s could not practically come to terms with new fiscal realities.

Finally, W. A. C. Bennett established the politics of personality as a major theme in B.C. public life. Leadership as an element in politics and in elections has probably been exaggerated by the news media in recent years. Today's voters cast their ballots as much for reasons of party affiliation, local issues, candidates or ideology as for individual political leaders. But in a time before the electronic news media dominated coverage of politics and public affairs, W. A. C. Bennett succeeded in focussing attention disproportionately on the personalities of leaders. By pitting his own flamboyant personality against those of struggling leaders of other parties, he won seven consecutive general elections and sent a legion of impressive opponents to ignominy. He fought issues, he argued policy, but most of all he demonstrated a genius for reducing complex political questions to a level everyone could understand: the character of the politician espousing the idea.

W. A. C. Bennett became as famous for his personality as for his achievements. And because his well-developed style dominated public life for so long, the politics of personality remains a dominant force in British Columbia. More than ideology and more than political philosophy, it is powerful personal loyalties, animosities and grudges that have shaped the province's development, its identity and its image abroad.

In the 1972 general election W. A. C. Bennett was elected for the eleventh consecutive time in his home riding of Okanagan South, but his Social Credit government was defeated. W. A. C. was the victim of his own successes, manifesting a weakness common among great political leaders: he hung on to power too long and did not give timely consideration to the question of leadership succession. In addition, so many years at the top produced in him a feeling of infallibility—he seemed to want to continue in power forever. But it was the social forces produced by the affluence and Good Life that W. A. C. had helped usher in that were largely responsible for his government's defeat. Change and progress left the aging premier behind, tempting the B.C. electorate to experiment with the political alternative.

The new premier, Dave Barrett, a generation younger than Bennett, had been an MLA for over a decade but had served as leader of the NDP for only a few years. (He never actually won a leadership convention; he finished second to Tom Berger in the leadership contest that preceded the 1969 B.C. election. When Berger then lost his own seat, the NDP caucus, preferring not to go through another messy, divisive leadership race, appointed Barrett party leader. This decision was subsequently endorsed at the party's regular annual convention.) Barrett was a political progeny of W. A. C. Bennett; like all other B.C. politicians of the era, he had learned at the feet of the populist master and had practised in his shadow. Barrett served as leader of the B.C. NDP for fifteen years. Too long.

After so many years of fighting against Social Credit and hurling abuse at the W. A. C. Bennett "dictatorship," the socialist hordes surprised themselves in 1972 by breaking down the gates. British Columbia in that year became the most affluent jurisdiction in North America ever to elect a socialist government. The NDP, however, never effectively managed to consolidate their power. First of all, they misinterpreted their mandate: they believed that the voters had directed them to implement socialism on Canada's west coast. The premier and his cabinet ineffectively promoted controversial new policies such as state-owned auto insurance, a provincial agricultural land reserve and new mineral royalties legislation with populist wording that was foreign to most British Columbians. Secondly, Dave Barrett was spooked by the legacies of his predecessor; he tried to emulate W. A. C. Bennett but was not up to the task. It was said that Barrett would have made a very good stand-up comic; the same could not be said for his talents as an impersonator. A social worker by training, Barrett even went so far as to retain the finance portfolio himself, as W. A. C. had done. Public servants in Victoria privately referred to the new premier as W. A. C. Barrett. However, Barrett simply could not run a W. A. C. Bennett—style government, let alone one with a very different political agenda.

The NDP administration was on the defensive almost from the start, and with Barrett trying to run a one-man show there was not much chance for co-ordination of policy or political team-building. Mistakes and $100 million "clerical errors" combined with a growing sense of political crisis in Victoria to create an overwhelming impression of administrative incompetence. Unwittingly, the novice NDP administration was managing to coalesce most non-socialist politicians against it. The provincial Liberals and Conservatives began to stir, and there was talk of forming a new provincial antisocialist party.

Meanwhile, many observers were saying that the somewhat demoralized Social Credit Party could not survive, for W. A. C. Bennett's retirement was imminent and there was no apparent successor. The 1972 election had seen the defeat of virtually every Socred cabinet minister or MLA who had either leadership aspirations or potential. W. A. C. encouraged his former attorney general, Les Peterson, to replace him, but Peterson was not prepared for the challenge. An earlier Socred heir-apparent, Robert Bonner, who had left Victoria for the corporate board room of MacMillan Bloedel, British Columbia's largest forest products company, was rumoured to be interested in returning to public life. W. A. C., however, publicly ruled him out for the leadership, explaining that Social Credit was "not a party of big business, but a party of all economic groups."

Calls for a nonpartisan unity party grew louder and louder, and moneyed interests seemed prepared to back such a new force. But the Social Credit Party's instinct for self-preservation was to be guarded by perhaps the only person in British Columbia with sufficient motivation for that daunting task: Bill Bennett, W. A. C.'s youngest son.

Having grown up with politics, Bill Bennett could not remember a specific time when he decided to follow in his father's footsteps. W. A. C. was, of course, a powerful role model. "The stimulating discussion in our family was about public affairs," recalled Bill. During his young adulthood, to test his commitment and his self-confidence, Bennett was active in community affairs in Kelowna; he joined Toastmasters to overcome an inability to express himself in public; he joined the chamber of commerce and became, at thirty-two, its youngest-ever local president. By the mid-1960s, believing that his father was about to retire, he readied himself to enter the political fray. But W. A. C. stayed on and on. By the time of the Social Credit defeat in 1972, forty-year-old Bill had almost given up. At a time when voters seemed to want young leaders, he feared that he might have missed his opportunity.

After that election, however, the younger Bennett's attitude towards public service changed. "When the government was defeated, I watched to see what was happening on the political spectrum," he said.

> I was very concerned. I was frightened for British Columbia and its economic prospects. And I was having a test of my confidence, as were the business community and a lot of us who were taking chances to build things for the future. That brought home to me that there were more than just philosophical goals. There was more than just personal commitment. There was a very real need to not only do the right thing but to prevent the wrong government getting in and the wrong thing from being done. You had to speak out.

With the Liberals and Conservatives jockeying for position with the Socreds in the ranks of the opposition, the Barrett government could remain comfortable. Efforts to form an antisocialist coalition of diverse interests dedicated to private enterprise were forestalled by the absence of a leader who could unite such disparate groups. Furthermore, Bill Bennett believed that only a strong, united Social Credit Party could regain power; coalitions, with their bickering and brokering, could never be successful in the long term.

Bennett sent a "Come home, we need you" telegram to his vacationing father, then off the coast of South Africa. W. A. C. immediately returned and tried to rally the Socred troops. The 72-year-old W. A. C., however, had no wish to stay on as leader, and when he confided his intention to resign his seat, Bill Bennett told his father that he would seek the nomination to replace him. "You really know what you're after and what you intend to do?" asked W. A. C. "Yes," replied his son, who also revealed that he wished to seek the party leadership. "He was supportive," said Bill Bennett. "I could tell he was pleased in his own way. I think he had hoped that someone from the family would run, and I knew he thought if anyone ran it would be me."

Bill Bennett had all of the necessary motives: he cared about the province, he was anxious about what was happening in Victoria, and he had a strong commitment to the Social Credit Party. "When I had joined the party as a young man of nineteen," he said, "it wasn't radical left, but it was a revolutionary movement that a young person could believe in. And it wasn't distasteful to my philosophy of private enterprise and individual rights; in fact, they were at the cornerstone of it. So it was something you could have fire in your belly about and something you could care about." Bill Bennett resented the assumption that the party was dead; he felt it was worth more than that.

In addition, he was motivated by family pride and pride in his father. "I wanted to work, to win, to help take some of the sting out of the defeat my father had suffered. This was the most powerful motive in the world." There could not have been another person in British Columbia at the time who carried such powerful impulses towards the task of reviving and rebuilding the Social Credit Party. Bennett would require all of this motivation and more to make his way through the obstacle course of B.C. politics.

Bill Bennett's first hurdle was the Okanagan South by-election of 7 September 1973 caused by W. A. C.'s formal retirement. It was a tough battle—the first campaign for a politician is usually the toughest—and despite being dismissed contemptuously as "daddy's little boy," Bill Bennett won. Suddenly this neophyte politician with the powerful surname was a leading contender for the Social Credit leadership to be decided in Vancouver that November.

The B.C. Socreds had never before experienced a leadership race. In 1952 they had run a leaderless campaign, and the party's

MLAs had voted W. A. C. Bennett leader and premier after their election win. Now, twenty-one years later, at a decisive time in the province's history, Social Credit would be choosing a new leader, and one capable, they hoped, of leading them back to power. Bill Bennett worked hard to prepare for the contest and was riding high as the newest Socred MLA but, unbeknownst to him, forces loyal to his father were busy behind the ramparts, ensuring that the party would make no mistake.

The Socred leadership race of 1973 culminated in British Columbia's first modern political leadership convention. All of the hoopla, banners and balloons made some of the fifteen hundred delegates a little uneasy; many of the party's old guard would undoubtedly have preferred the convention take place in a church basement.

The chief contender to Bill Bennett was freshman Langley MLA Bob McClelland, who was not alone in feeling that he stood a strong chance. Hugh Harris, who had managed Bill Bennett's by-election victory and was now in charge of his leadership campaign, was asked whom he would like to see win if Bennett did not make it. He responded that, next to his man, McClelland would make the best leader. (Bennett later shouted at Harris: "We don't ever concede defeat!")

As it turned out, there was not much of a contest. Bennett said:

We had no provision in my campaign for what to do beyond the first ballot. In my whole organization we had never discussed it. We were going there to win—I was going there to win. I would have felt devastated if I thought I was everybody's fifth choice. I went to be their first choice. And in fact at that convention there was no drama. They had a big electric sign in the theatre that showed the changing totals as they counted the ballots in the back room. I'm told that in order to keep some suspense they tried to hold up some of my votes.

Bill Bennett won on the first ballot with 883 votes. McClelland received the support of 269 delegates. Of equal importance for the rejuvenating Socreds was the election of a new party president. Grace McCarthy, formerly a Socred cabinet minister, won the position with the visible support of W. A. C. Bennett. Her organizational talents and political fervour would profit Social Credit in the crucial months ahead.

For Grace McCarthy the purpose of the convention went well beyond electing a new leader. The point of the exercise was to demonstrate that the Social Credit Party was alive and well, contrary to the assertions of those who wanted to start a new political party. "That was the show," recalled McCarthy. "That was the motivation. But it wasn't a race."

Within British Columbia a new chapter in the politics of personality was being written, with strong overtones of popular psychology and dynastic intrigue. Bill Bennett would go out of his way to distance himself from his father, determined to live up to the challenge of leadership by sheer hard work despite whispers of nepotism. In his victory speech he was emphatic: "Let it be clearly understood by friend and foe alike that as your new leader I am my own man."

Nevertheless, his father would be at once his greatest liability and his most important asset. While the greenhorn opposition leader learned the ropes in the legislature, suffering the taunts and jeers of more experienced politicians, the former premier engaged himself in a travelling Socred road show geared towards rallying the faithful and signing up new members. Touring the province with the hauteur of a fallen monarch, the elder Bennett was accompanied by the enthusiastic Grace McCarthy, whom he dubbed "British Columbia's number one freedom fighter," and another former cabinet minister, "Dangerous Dan" Campbell. The energetic trio perfected a routine of bashing the NDP government, preaching against socialism and selling Socred memberships like bubble-gum cards. W. A. C. had left the party in poor shape in 1972, with only a few thousand members and virtually no organization. Now, through a concerted effort and a kind of religious zeal, the Social Credit Party could soon boast the largest membership of any provincial political organization in Canada. "Amazing Grace" McCarthy peddled 32,000 party memberships in 1974 alone, and by the time of the next election she could point to a strongly revitalized party with more than 70,000 signed-up, born-again Socreds.

But it was no mean feat to establish Social Credit as the only plausible alternative to the NDP government. Bill Bennett was new on the political stage, and most British Columbians were unconvinced that he could resurrect the Social Credit Party and lead it as his father had. Graham Lea, then an NDP cabinet minister, recalled that Bill Bennett was not taken seriously: "He was a hick. They literally had to take him out of his white shoes and fortrel at Hope and shove him into a wool suit before they brought him into town."

Acceptance and recognition in Vancouver, the media and business centre of British Columbia, would always prove difficult for Bill Bennett, but never more so than when he was the struggling, tentative leader of the opposition. Mike Burns, an IBM vice-president who was new to British Columbia and apprehensive about the directions of the left-wing government, began asking senior Vancouver business executives about Bennett's prospects and met with a largely noncommittal response. Burns quietly arranged a luncheon with Bennett and some of those executives—many of them third and fourth generation British Columbians, senior business people who had never met Bennett—at a Vancouver hotel. After the meal the waiters were sent from the room, and the businessmen, Burns said, launched into Bennett:

> "Who the hell are you? You're just your father's son. Is he really running the show? Can you really stand up to this?" And he answered sincerely and actually impressed them. He impressed them as a tough guy who knew where he was going. And everybody was really a bit taken aback. You could see the quandary on their faces: "What do we do now?"
>
> And when it was over Grace McCarthy stood up, and she gave these guys shit. She said: "You sign these membership cards right now, and you work." And some of those guys did. And I did. I was hooked.

Such meetings among the Vancouver business community were important, but the emergence of Bill Bennett and Social Credit owed more to the Socred revival that McCarthy, Campbell and others organized province-wide. And the juggernaut became irresistible when prominent members of other parties began defecting to the Social Credit team: in mid-1974 Tory MLA Hugh Curtis signed on, as did Conservative Party president Peter Hyndman. Then Bill Vander Zalm, a well-known Liberal and the popular mayor of Surrey, came on board.

By the following year Bill Bennett was taking more effective control of a political party that was being dynamically transformed.

When, by late 1975, it was abundantly clear that no new force would or could replace Social Credit as the alternative to the socialist government, three Liberal MLAs, Allan Williams, Pat McGeer and Garde Gardom, joined Social Credit. Bill Bennett said: "In business, when you want to expand, you use one company as a vehicle. You naturally choose the one with the broadest base and the best-known name." In spite of being completely written off in the aftermath of its 1972 defeat, by 1975 Social Credit had become the sought-after unity party—without changing the name of the old family firm.

Now the motivation to dislodge the NDP from Victoria was almost frantic. Far from allaying the generations-old nightmares of antisocialists, the Barrett administration spawned new fears almost daily. Farmers complained that they were being made serfs on their own land; developers and development capital fled the province; the mining industry, protesting against the new mineral royalties legislation, came to a virtual halt; private insurance companies howled in protest against the new Insurance Corporation of British Columbia. The NDP government, venturing into the world of business with little hesitation, established several other crown corporations. It blocked the transfer of forest tenure to interests outside the province and purchased sawmills and pulp mills, including those owned by Columbia Cellulose, Kootenay Forest Products, Plateau Mills and Ocean Falls. It acquired companies active in real estate and public transport and even purchased a poultry operation. Reaction to these initiatives was generally hostile, and the Barrett government, sensitive to the criticism, passed up what could have been its biggest coup: the takeover of Pacific Western Airlines. While Barrett hesitated, the airline was purchased by the Alberta Conservative government.

It was not so much *what* the NDP administration did as how it was done that caused the party's most serious difficulties. Their strident socialist rhetoric, their combative media relations and their overly defensive leader inspired a general lack of confidence. Premier Barrett, who could be an extremely compelling orator, continued to behave as if he was leader of the opposition. Furthermore, he had succumbed to the rising expectations of the W. A. C. Bennett era by giving in: the civil service grew by 28 per cent and became extremely politicized; public sector salaries increased as much as 56 per cent, leading the private sector; even MLAs' salaries were substantially raised. All of this contributed, in the vulnerable B.C. economy, to an inflationary spiral. Late in 1975 Dave Barrett relinquished the finance portfolio, likely recognizing that he had both underestimated expenditures and overestimated revenues. By 1975 the NDP experiment in power resembled a hangover following a wild binge on the Good Life.

One of the Barrett government's thorniest problems was dealing with a prime NDP constituency: organized labour. In the eyes of the trade union leadership, great strides were made during the Barrett regime in such areas as collective bargaining and the right to strike. The labour bosses had high expectations, however, and their satisfaction with Victoria's policies diminished as time went by. An increase in the number of labour disputes was a source of embarrassment for the government. Barrett was forced to struggle with the paradox of socialism in power. In October 1975, after a summer of crippling strikes, he confronted British Columbia's militant labour leadership and ordered workers in the pulp and paper industry back to work. Then, in an emergency session of the legislature, the NDP government passed legislation ordering striking workers in major food retail chains back to their jobs. The unions cried "betrayal" and "treachery," while Barrett, basking in the imaginary glow of strong leadership, mulled over the prospect of a snap election. The NDP cabinet was split on the issue. Graham Lea, then an NDP minister, recalled:

To some extent it broke down into who thought they could win their own seat and who couldn't. [Provincial Secretary] Ernie Hall and I were going over to a meeting at Barrett's house, and I was in favour of calling an election and Ernie was against it. At that time cabinet ministers made, with their MLA's wages, $48,000 a year. I said to Ernie: "Give me one reason why we shouldn't call the election now." He said: "I'll give you 48,000 reasons!"

Barrett made the decision on his own. The showdown with the unions had firmed his resolve; in addition, he knew that the government was heading for a deficit, which in British Columbia's political vocabulary was a dirty word. Although he and his party had been severe critics of W. A. C. Bennett's practice of going to the polls every three to three and a half years, Barrett stuck to yet another tradition of his political mentor and announced a general election for 11 December 1975.

The Liberals and Conservatives ran slates of mostly half-hearted candidates. Virtually everyone conceded that the campaign was a battle between Barrett's socialists and the new Socreds under Bill Bennett, a tense and dramatic contest between two belligerent factions, each taking the paranoid style of B.C. politics to new heights.

The NDP campaign centred on the leadership of Dave Barrett and little else. He delivered bravura performances at meeting after meeting, turning the election campaign into a kind of vaudeville contest which might possibly be won on the basis of personal showmanship. However, the laughter and hoopla sometimes verged on unease and fear. The NDP, the party that prided itself on policy and ideas, had seemingly exhausted itself after only a little more than three years in power. The socialists had been reduced to a leader—"Fat Little Dave Barrett"—and the leader to a paranoid slogan—"Don't let them take it away!"

The Socred campaign got off to a shaky start, with Bill Bennett cold and nervous compared to the flamboyant Barrett. W. A. C. Bennett, sympathetic to his son's striving to be his own man, stayed completely out of the limelight. The younger Bennett wisely refused to appear in a televised debate with Barrett, who would easily have taken advantage of his inexperience. Instead he travelled the province, attacking socialist mismanagement and spouting the slogan "Let's get B.C. moving again!"

As election day drew closer, some pundits felt that Barrett, playing a variation on a theme established by W. A. C. Bennett as the persecuted loner, might just squeak back in on a tide of sympathy. But in a glaring exception to the inherent fairness of voters who will give most new governments a second chance, Social Credit racked up almost 50 per cent of the province's popular vote, taking thirty-five seats in the legislature. The remaining seats were divided among eighteen New Democrats, one Liberal and one Conservative. Dave Barrett suffered a personal, humiliating defeat at the hands of Socred George Kerster, a little-known car dealer in his home riding of Coquitlam.

On election night at the Social Credit campaign headquarters in

Kelowna, the loudest cheers and applause were reserved for
W. A. C. Bennett, who always said that revenge was best eaten
cold. Seventy-five-year-old Wacky was simultaneously laughing
and crying as he told the hysterical crowd: "Now a people's government is back in power and everybody can breathe easier
tonight. There have been three and a half years in the wilderness
for the people, and that's too long. I said in the past that people
need to put their finger on the hot stove of socialism. They felt it.
Now they've taken their finger away." If it had not been for the
NDP interregnum, the Bennett dynasty would never have been
possible. It was W. A. C. Bennett's 1972 defeat that paved the way
for his son and a unique kind of personal vengeance in 1975. The
political succession was neither well planned nor cleanly executed,
but for the Bennetts it was sweet.

Many years earlier, when W. A. C. Bennett became premier, he
had moved to Victoria, leaving his sons Bill and R. J. to take care
of his business. The brothers did as their father asked and, in addition, developed successful businesses of their own. Bill Bennett
now faced the daunting challenge of taking charge of the provincial
government; he asked R. J. to take care of his business interests,
recognizing that running the government was going to be a full-
time commitment. In fact, it would be a larger task than Bennett
then realized. His background was that of a small businessman, an
entrepreneur; he had never run a large organization and had little
experience with the world of big business.

In his crash course in management and administration, the premier had the help of his fourteen hand-picked cabinet colleagues:
Grace McCarthy became provincial secretary, minister of tourism
and, significantly, deputy premier; Bill Vander Zalm was appointed to the sensitive post of human resources, whose minister
would never win a popularity contest; Bennett would not contem-
plate retaining finance for himself and gave that responsibility to
Evan Wolfe, a car dealer; another Socred car dealer, Don Phillips,
received the dual portfolios of economic development and agriculture; Pat McGeer became minister of education; Garde Gardom
was attorney general; Allan Williams was minister of labour; former
Tory Hugh Curtis received the portfolios of municipal affairs and
housing; Jim Nielsen, formerly a radio hotliner, filled the new post
of minister of environment; Jack Davis, who had been a federal

Liberal cabinet minister, became transportation and communications minister; Alex Fraser was picked for highways; Socred leadership runner-up Bob McClelland became health minister; Rafe Mair, a lawyer from Kamloops, was appointed to consumer affairs; and Tom Waterland, a mining engineer, received the forests and resources portfolios.

British Columbia's new executive council was notable for an abundance of political talents but a paucity of experience in provincial government. Yet like their leader most had strong points of view about the tasks they were entering into. At the cabinet swearing-in ceremony, Bill Vander Zalm set the tone for a new direction when he remarked: "If anybody is able to work, but refuses to pick up the shovel, we will find ways of dealing with him."

Bill Bennett was denied the honeymoon period customarily accorded to new premiers. From his first day in office he faced intense criticism. So continually was he derided as "daddy's little boy" that he must have sometimes doubted whether he was in fact his own man. Even the first cabinet meeting was marred by a demonstration: unemployed protesters wielding shovels burst into the cabinet room—a graphic response to Vander Zalm's controversial "shovel" statement.

Right from the start Bill Bennett acquired a reputation for being remote and distant. His personality mirrored his lifestyle: he was a very private, shy individual coming into office through an unusual route, with special motivations. He believed he could not afford to befriend his colleagues, remembering his father's advice: "Make lots of friends, but don't get to know any of them too closely." The practical aspects of running a government were learned by trial and error while he attempted to consolidate his power as party leader. These lessons were tougher for Bennett, who had never spent time in government and who was under close public, media and opposition scrutiny.

> I even had to learn to know my colleagues. We had rebuilt the party
> so fast with all these people, and we didn't know each other. We
> had no history with each other. A lot of them had antagonisms that
> they carried with them from before when they were in different
> parties, and now they were all in the same tent. I had to learn all
> that, and I had to learn it in public.

Bennett may have made the experience more painful than necessary by trying so rebelliously to be his own man. Believing that any perceived influence by his father would have a negative political effect, Bill Bennett did not permit W. A. C. to come close to the practice of power. He found it difficult during his first years in office to even acknowledge his father's contribution and referred to him in public only as "the former member for Okanagan South." Even so, there were suggestions that the younger Bennett was a wooden man controlled by his ventriloquist father in Kelowna. It was hinted that he ran home on weekends for advice. Later, Bill Bennett explained that his behaviour was not a sign of insecurity. Many Liberals and Conservatives who might support Social Credit, he said, did not want another W. A. C. Bennett. "They had to know that there was a difference and that they had a chance. And, therefore, it was good politics."

Bill Bennett also avoided most of the old-guard Socreds and studiously ignored W. A. C.'s cronies. The few acknowledgements he made to paternal influence were essentially practical decisions: Robert Bonner, W. A. C.'s attorney general, was appointed chairman of B.C. Hydro; Dan Campbell, another W. A. C. Bennett minister, received a senior civil service appointment in Intergovernmental Affairs, and Grace McCarthy—who, politically, was more a daughter to W. A. C. than Bill was a son—received her senior cabinet posts.

During the early part of Bill Bennett's premiership, his office was exceptionally understaffed, and he mastered the transition to government virtually by himself. His childhood friend Tony Tozer became his first executive assistant, and he had a press secretary. Lawrie Wallace returned from his post as British Columbia's agent general in London to serve for a short while as the premier's deputy minister. Bennett may also have been interested in retaining a senior NDP government adviser, Mark Eliesen, to help set up the administration's cabinet system. Eliesen, or "the Rabbi" as he was nicknamed, had come to British Columbia during the late stage of the Barrett administration to serve as a planning adviser to cabinet. However, upon the defeat of the NDP government he automatically resigned and left the province to pursue socialist causes elsewhere.

Nevertheless, the novice premier quickly set to work differentiating his government from both the Barrett regime and the pre-

1972 Socreds. It is Bill Bennett who brought modern government to British Columbia, with planning and policy co-ordination at the cabinet level, a functional cabinet committee system and all of the offices, commissions and agencies necessary to lock horns with other provincial and federal bureaucracies. While running for the Social Credit leadership, Bennett had talked of liberalizing the party; as opposition leader and during the election he spoke of modernizing government. Now he was making fundamental changes to the machinery of public administration in British Columbia. Government would continue to grow, as it had under NDP auspices, but now, it was hoped, its expansion would be controlled. In addition, progressive features common in other jurisdictions would be introduced: an auditor general to serve as an independent watchdog on government spending, an ombudsman to investigate citizens' grievances against government, and even an all-party legislative committee on crown corporations to scrutinize the activities of public enterprises.

Even though his administration was the first to break away from the simple and crude government machinery it had inherited, Bill Bennett was derisively referred to as "Mini-Wac." Yet in terms of style and decision making, it was Dave Barrett who had played the role of Mini-Wac. Bill Bennett's regime, on the other hand, was building up a large, highly technocratic organization that was consistent with other colourless Canadian governments and in many respects incompatible with the nature and style of B.C. politics. It almost seemed as if the era of flamboyant, populist leadership was finished in British Columbia.

Compared with the tumult of the Barrett years, Bill Bennett's first term was relatively quiet. Much effort was made to discredit the previous administration, and several reports were issued testifying to NDP mismanagement. B.C. politics would be nothing without scandal, and Bennett's government suffered a few early embarrassments: Speaker Ed Smith was forced to resign when it was revealed that he had used his influence to obtain a job for a young woman friend in the new office of the auditor general. Even more distressing was the forced resignation of cabinet minister Jack Davis in 1978 after it was found that he had purchased first class airline tickets to travel on government business and then traded them in for economy class, pocketing the difference. The former cabinet colleague of Pierre Trudeau was found guilty of fraud; he continued as an MLA but never again served in the cabinet of Bill Bennett.

Perhaps the political highlight of Bennett's first term in office was also his only notable populist flourish. Late in 1978 he descended from an Okanagan ski hill to announce: "B.C. is not for sale." He was responding to a proposed takeover of the province's forest industry giant, MacMillan Bloedel, by eastern Canadian–based Canadian Pacific. The premier indicated that he would do everything in his power to block the sale of the B.C. company to this out-of-province interest; after all, the Canadian Pacific Railway was historically the most hated corporation in all of western Canada. Bennett's efforts did force Canadian Pacific to back off, signifying a political victory for the Social Credit government. But for a man strongly committed to the virtues of private enterprise and less government interference in the marketplace, the premier's statement was a strange one. Populism is not without its contradictions.

In retrospect, with continuing changes in the ownership of many large provincial corporations, "B.C. is not for sale" rings hollow. But in 1978 British Columbia was still enjoying the Good Life. Through the NDP years and well into the new premier's stewardship, while the provincial economy was showing signs of volatility and instability, prices for B.C. commodities—lumber, pulp and paper, coal, minerals, natural gas—were rising. British Columbians were producing products that were greatly in demand throughout the world. And B.C., therefore, was not for sale.

This economic backdrop formed the basis for what was perhaps the most innovative public policy initiative of the period. In 1977 the Socred administration introduced legislation to create the private British Columbia Resources Investment Corporation (BCRIC). "Brick," as it came to be known, would be made up primarily of assets acquired by the NDP administration and would fulfil a 1975 Social Credit election plank to denationalize government-owned companies. This was the first significant Canadian experiment in privatization and was structured to encourage British Columbians to invest in the future development of the province through share ownership in BCRIC. In January of 1979 Bennett announced that the government would distribute five free BCRIC shares to every man, woman and child in British Columbia—thus everyone would own "a piece of the rock." Canadian citizens were eligible to purchase more shares, providing additional capitalization for the company to expand, diversify and, with luck, create jobs. Declared Bennett: "This is the commitment of our government to individual ownership rather than socialism or government ownership."

The BCRIC idea had a boldness reminiscent of some of the actions of W. A. C. Bennett. During these years, the elder Bennett, making few ventures into the public limelight, was privately critical of many of the government's actions and from time to time tried to feed helpful suggestions to cabinet ministers. He believed his son was surrounding himself with too many yes-men, and he laughed at the assertion that a "modern" government was being established in Victoria. "Government is not complicated," he would say. "Only people make it complicated." W. A. C. Bennett's death on 23 February 1979 concluded a remarkable personal saga and in a very real way marked the end of an era in British Columbia.

Bill Bennett was finally free to prove himself and his ultimate worth. Planning for a general election had already commenced with a cabinet shuffle in late 1978. The most significant changes included the controversial, attention-getting Bill Vander Zalm taking charge of Municipal Affairs; he was replaced at Human Resources by the indefatigable Grace McCarthy. When McCarthy had become a cabinet minister following the 1975 election, her official involvement with the Social Credit Party organization ended. Now the experienced political warhorse, Dan Campbell, emerged as the leading Socred organizer for the forthcoming electoral battle. Along the way, Bill Bennett met the federal Liberals' chief pollster, Martin Goldfarb, and commissioned him to undertake some public opinion research for the government. Bennett struck up a strong personal rapport with Goldfarb, who later conducted the basic preparatory polling for the party leading up to the election that Bennett called for 10 May 1979.

The election was a hard-fought campaign, once again pitting the two party leaders from 1975 against each other. The personal animosity between Barrett and Bennett infected the election and poisoned the rhetoric of both parties. Bennett kicked off the campaign by proclaiming that it was a necessary contest to determine whether British Columbians preferred individual ownership, as represented by the Socred government's plan to give away free shares in BCRIC, or state ownership under the NDP. "People must be given a choice, and it's a clear choice," he declared. He referred to the New Democrats as the party advocating "national social-ism," a reference that was played up by the news media and drove Barrett to distraction. The first Jewish premier in Canadian history believed that Bennett was baiting him with the term "national socialists"—the official name of Hitler's Nazis.

The strange campaign coincided with labour-dispute disruptions of Vancouver's daily newspapers, overlapped a federal election campaign and competed for attention with the Stanley Cup play-offs. The NDP camp was as usual well organized—there was never any doubt about their impressive political machine's ability to get out their vote. By contrast the Social Credit campaign was poorly organized and ineffective; it seemed to rely too strongly on the belief that voters would not gamble again with socialism.

In spite of this, the Socreds won a slim majority—thirty-one seats to twenty-six for the NDP—and the two parties' popular vote was almost even. (The Liberals and Conservatives were com-pletely shut out; polarization was now complete.) Although Bill Bennett declared that a victory is a victory whether by an inch or by a mile, the closeness of the election results would generate con-siderable activity on his part during the course of this new, narrow mandate.

It was not until a few months after the election dust had settled that it was revealed just how inept and disorganized the Socred campaign had been. If the revelations and allegations of political impropriety and wrongdoing had emerged prior to the election, the government would have gone down to a shattering defeat. First there was the "Dirty Tricks" affair, or "Lettergate" as the media dubbed it, in which amateur Socred organizers had advised party workers in the crude arts of deception. The dirty tricks included writing to editors of B.C. newspapers letters praising the Socreds, attacking the NDP, and signed with fictitious names. Such advice was packaged as part of a widely distributed audio-cassette campaign kit. It was also reported that campaign chairman Dan Campbell had been seen handing out thousand-dollar bills to party workers, and that over $60,000 in Socred expenses was un-accounted for. Later there were charges of gerrymandering, allega-tions that the Socreds had influenced the Electoral Reform Com-mission, resulting in alterations to constituency boundaries and two additional ridings being represented in the House. This was the "Gracie's Finger" affair, so named after the small digit-shaped section on the electoral map that was added to Grace McCarthy's riding of Vancouver—Little Mountain. Noting that the new, strongly Socred portion of the constituency resembled an upright finger, Dave Barrett, in his inimitable style, branded it "political pornography."

All of these scandals, charges and innuendoes created a sense of political crisis in Victoria and a strong feeling that the newly elected Social Credit administration was corrupt. This in turn produced a defensive, backpedalling reaction from the government, resulting in a deep-seated malaise as well as a period of inactivity in public policy. It was in this extremely difficult environment that Bill Bennett, sensing how tenuous his hold on power actually was, began to redirect his political party and assert his leadership over it. He had managed to win two general elections as party leader without ever involving himself deeply in party matters. Now came the harsh realization that party leadership was at least as important as government leadership; he would not be able to lead the province if he could not master his party. Consequently he established new priorities: his first term in office had been devoted to modernizing government; his second term would focus on modernizing and making professional the Social Credit Party, turning it into an institution that could survive any single leader. The party had never had an executive director or officers, and it had been left to the party president and the directors to organize for electoral battles. Bennett saw the need for trained personnel, for organization and for more modern techniques.

Mike Burns, who was involved in the Social Credit campaign of 1979 and would become Bill Bennett's link to the Vancouver business community, said:

> When it came time to fight the election in '79, Bill Bennett had never been through one that he had anything to do with. In '75 they did it to him, or *for* him, and he basically said, "Do it again." So they bashed some of the pieces together, which wasn't very much because it had really fallen apart. It was a real mess. They put together a team of old hacks, a lot of drinking in the headquarters. It was called Ice Station Zebra, and it was just out of the comic books. So the election was won in the constituencies—but *just*—because

the central campaign had very little going for it. It was a shock for Bill Bennett. And then he took over. He hired Hugh Harris.

Hugh Harris had managed Bill Bennett's first by-election victory and had run his successful leadership campaign as well, and the premier trusted his expertise in organization and entrepreneurship. Harris accepted the position of executive director of the Social Credit Party, and after a quick tour of most provincial ridings he reported to Bennett on the need for broad change. Mike Burns, who was about to become the chief party fund raiser, remembered meeting with Bennett and Harris and telling them that there were a lot of modern-day political methods the party should be using. Bennett said the party could not afford to do those things.

My rejoinder was: "We can't afford to do less. If you want to stay in office, there's no alternative." Bennett said: "Well, what do you do if you don't have the money?" I said—my most foolish statement ever, probably—"I'll guarantee you lack of money will never be an excuse for not doing it right." And so we just agreed. We would do what we had to to get the best of everything to do it right.

And so with Harris spearheading the drive, the Social Credit Party was significantly shaken up and remoulded. Bennett said:

We started to build the organization and get some political expertise, and we had lots of fights with the party in trying to get them to accept this discipline. I became the referee. Various people from both sides, including Hugh, were going to quit at various times. But it had to be done. And it was done with a certain amount of pain because it was a dramatic change in the party. Hiring organizers, building the organization in the constituencies, making it work. We had lots of members—it was just making it work and letting everybody know why they were doing certain things and letting them know about the new campaign techniques.

Bennett sent Hugh Harris to study political organizations. Harris's wanderings throughout North America in 1979 and 1980 brought him into contact with the best and brightest organizers, masters of assessing and influencing the moods of electorates. Although he picked up ideas from many different sources, the organization that most impressed him was the Ontario Progressive Conservative Party, the Big Blue Machine that had sustained Tory administrations in that province for forty years. In 1981 he hired the first of the recruits from the Big Blue Machine, a young organizer named Jerry Lampert. Lampert could not at first believe how little the Social Credit Party had organized:

> I was astounded at the lack of a modern fundraising program that got money through the direct mail process or even in a systematic way from the corporations. I have been told stories—I don't know how true they are—that when a campaign happened, one person would go to MacMillan Bloedel and say "Write the cheque." And they did! There was no systematic approach to it. There was little or no activity between elections.
>
> And I heard all the horror stories from Hugh about the 1979 election, like the day they took off and literally did circles in the air because no one knew where they were going. They were arguing about where they should go, and then they finally went. And then when they landed, no one knew they were coming, so there was nothing prepared to greet them. There were stories about them having two aircraft, and the premier's party was travelling in an aircraft that went a lot faster than the second plane that was carrying the media, so they kept getting to events before the media even arrived. So, of course, there was no coverage.

Lampert was invited to a meeting in Kelowna with Bennett, Hugh Harris, Allan Gregg, the Tories' chief pollster, and Nancy McLean, one of Canada's best-known political image makers, to discuss preparations for the next election campaign.

> Before we went in we had an early morning breakfast with Allen and Nancy. And if you know Nancy McLean, she has quite a mouth on her. She can talk with the best of them, swear with the best of them. Hugh said: "Look, Bennett's pretty straightlaced. You've really got to watch what you say. He doesn't like swearing. So let's be really cool." So we go into the meeting and Allan gives his presentation and, of course, it's superb—it was on political polling, what polling is, what it can do for Bennett as leader, how it can be used, how he can feel comfortable with it. And then Nancy does her thing about

how she takes that polling information and helps portray a political image, helps a leader position himself to be perceived by the public in a certain way. Hugh and I are on edge through the whole thing— we're waiting for her to trip over her tongue and say something profane. And she goes through the whole thing and she's summing up and we're saying to ourselves, "We made it!" And right at the end, the very last thing she said was: "Premier, what I do is I get all the people in a circle, and I get them all pissing out of the tent instead of pissing *in*to the tent." And Bennett's jaw dropped. And Hugh and I covered our faces.

Bennett quickly recovered, and the session proceeded well. The next day Harris held a small gathering at his cottage on Lake Okanagan. Lampert remembered sitting on the dock with Mike Burns and a few others, thinking about ways to overcome Bennett's difficult public image. "All of a sudden this speedboat comes along, and there's Bennett, stripped to the waist, tanned, in good shape, sunglasses on. And Audrey's sitting beside him. And he pulls up to the dock. I thought, 'Shit, if we could ever get that on camera . . .' "

Jerry Lampert joined the Social Credit Party in July 1981 as director of operations. A few months later Hugh Harris recruited Lampert's former boss from Ontario's Big Blue Machine, Patrick Kinsella, to help with the premier's "difficult image." Kinsella, who once described himself as "the best political hack in the country," was initially appointed—against his wishes and better judgement—deputy minister to the premier. For all of his political genius, Kinsella would never successfully adapt to British Columbia's unique populist culture, and his struggles to change Bill Bennett's image would also meet with failure. Nevertheless, beginning in the fall of 1981 he, Lampert, Harris and a coterie of others would build an impressive political machine, unrivalled by any party organization in Canada, even the Big Blue Machine.

It was all paid for by the party's new fundraising arm, run by Mike Burns, who made good on his promise to the premier that "lack of money would never be an excuse for not doing it right." In addition to its continued base of personal membership fees and individual donations, the party built an aggressive fundraising machine that targeted British Columbia's business community, and particularly large corporations. Conceived by Burns and Harris in 1980, the exclusive business/political fraternity known as the Top 20 remained a closely kept secret for several years. Burns remembered:

> We knew we had twenty swing ridings in the province where we'd won or lost by 10 per cent or less. If we were going to win the next election, we had to win those.
>
> We wanted to get some people involved and we wanted to raise some money. So we said: "Okay, we'll get twenty guys to be the mother hens—twenty top business guys for those twenty ridings."
>
> Hugh Harris said: "Yeah, that's okay."
>
> "What do we hit them for?"
>
> "We hit them for five grand a year."
>
> "It's hardly worth organizing for a hundred grand."
>
> "Why don't we have three guys for each constituency?"
>
> And Harris said: "Okay."
>
> So now I'm happier. I've got three hundred grand from these guys. But who knows if the dogs are going to eat this? The guys had never done this before.

The first meeting was attended by about forty-five top business people who, Burns said, shared the Socreds' fear that they wouldn't make it through the next election, and they wanted to help. But beyond giving money, they wanted to get involved. Burns knew they were too busy to truly be involved; he also knew that "if they gave us the dough and pretended they would work, we could go and buy the workers and leave them as enthusiastic amateurs to be there."

Initially, the members of the Top 20 looked for nothing back except an ability to maintain the government in office. It was up to Burns to keep them interested:

> We gave them up-to-date information. We would arrange briefings for them with various ministers. For example, right after the budget speech we'd have the finance minister come over and sit with them over lunch and tell them what the budget really meant. "Here's what I was trying to do. Here's why I didn't do this or that." Nothing sacrosanct, just a touchy-feely.
>
> The other thing we gave them was access to as many events as we could. Whatever was going down, when we were renting a crowd,

they were in the front row. It was good for everybody—it reflected well on the event, it reflected well on the government. And it made these guys—most of whom were prominent in their own right and would have been on the list—feel that they were respected, revered and wanted.

Top 20 was Bennett's link to the business community. Burns said: "He developed a high level of trust with these guys, so that all you had to say was, 'He's a Top 20 guy, and he'd like to see you.' Or 'He'd like to send you a note on the subject.' Or 'He'd like a hearing on something.' Or 'He's got an idea.' Then there was dialogue without the preliminaries."

So, with Hugh Harris's recruitment program in place, Jerry Lampert whipping the Socred Party into shape, Pat Kinsella trying to work his magic in Victoria and Mike Burns keeping the party coffers filled in Vancouver, the formula for political success seemed to have been found.

As his second term as premier unfolded, Bill Bennett faced some severe challenges. Most important was a deepening recession in British Columbia that would colour government policy in far-reaching ways. All resource companies in the province were affected by the recession, including the floundering BCRIC. The investment community and the broad base of shareholders were openly critical of the now-private company's management, and the share value was dropping sharply. The privatization process, however, had been a success, even if many shareholders wrongly suspected that the government was still involved in BCRIC's management.

While Bennett struggled to rebuild his party, his government seemed to come unglued. The "Dirty Tricks" scandal and "Gracie's Finger" affair were not isolated incidents. Cabinet ministers Bob McClelland and Hugh Curtis, in separate trips to New York City, indulged in expensive hotels, limousines and theatre tickets at public expense. A public review of the ministers' expense accounts embarrassed the government at a time when the premier was speaking seriously about the need to cut back on public spending. An earlier expense account scandal had caused the resignation of a new and promising cabinet minister, Peter Hyndman. Documents relayed by the NDP to the press revealed, amongst other indiscretions, a dinner for six at taxpayers' expense, during which four bottles of expensive French wine were consumed.

At the time, such events so severely tarnished the Bennett administration's credibility that most observers believed the government's days were numbered. The premier moved swiftly to gain firmer control of his government. Leashes on his ministers were shortened; the authority of the premier's office was increased. Powerful pressures and antagonisms among his colleagues resulted, but Bill Bennett was determined to assert his leadership. One cabinet minister resigned—Rafe Mair left in 1981—and other ministers pondered resignation. Several ministers did in fact submit their resignations to Bennett, who declined to accept them.

An incident in July 1982 revealed some of the mounting tensions within the Social Credit cabinet and held significance for the future. Municipal Affairs Minister Bill Vander Zalm had been trying for more than two years to obtain the necessary approvals for the land use bill, a widely discussed bill that was the focus of rising political opposition from municipalities and special interest groups. It proposed a radical restructuring of local government in British Columbia, concentrating enormous power in the hands of the minister and abolishing the Islands Trust, the elected body empowered to preserve the Gulf Islands from large-scale real estate development. Vander Zalm had committed himself to passage of the bill and had stood up to all the criticism. The cabinet was of the view that the bill was too hot to handle, and, looking at the possibility of a fall election, the premier felt it was easier to adjourn the House and let the bill die on the order paper than to prolong the legislative session with yet another controversy.

Vander Zalm sank into an uncharacteristic depression. The cabinet's last-moment decision would constitute a major loss of face for him. He seriously considered resigning—"Not because I lost, but because of the way it was handled"—and he called a news conference with that in mind.

Derek De Biasio, Vander Zalm's executive assistant and policy co-ordinator, recalled:

> Vander Zalm did not want to resign, but he was very, very frustrated. And you have few options in that kind of a situation —resignation is one of them. And the fact that he was being forced to consider that option also frustrated him. It was one of those situa-

tions that just popped up. The premier just brought it to a head one moment and then Vander Zalm had to start thinking about what he was going to do the next moment. There was no real time to think things out. It was quite a dramatic moment.

Word quickly travelled within the parliament buildings; colleagues and fellow ministers pleaded with him to stay and fight another day. Relenting, he went through with his news conference, but instead of resigning he castigated the premier and cabinet, calling them "gutless." Vander Zalm said:

I had to find a way through it all. I thought, "If I'm not going to resign from this, I don't want to have it appear as though I backed away." Because I had fought it through all the committees, I'd gone through the whole of the process, agonizing night after night, day after day, weekends, for months on end. And I'd been promoting it throughout the various communities with municipal groups and community groups. So I really not only felt let down by all of this, but it felt necessary for me to somehow subtly, but effectively, get the message out that it wasn't me that called it quits.

Far from being subtle, Vander Zalm's "gutless" comment was the most significant public breach of cabinet solidarity experienced during Bill Bennett's administration. The premier now had to fight against the impression that his cabinet was in a state of revolt. He responded by tightening procedures, closing up communication gaps and ensuring that no individual minister's policy making ever strayed too far from the cabinet table. "If government is a team," Bennett said, "policy comes from the cabinet table—it should not be personalized. That's a danger of not having policy as *government* policy."

Perhaps one important act prevented Vander Zalm from leaving government. Grace McCarthy visited him in his office during the crucial moments when he was contemplating resigning. She attempted to change his mind, tried to buoy his sagging spirits and left him with these fateful words: "Remember what W. A. C. Bennett used to say: 'Don't get mad. Get even.' "

CHAPTER 2

Good and Bad British Columbians

Canadian provincial politics are *provincial* politics. This is the nature of Canadian federalism. A provincial premier necessarily feeds on and gives expression to local pride, strong regional grievances and popular prejudices. Most provinces flaunt their powers and flex their politics as if they were autonomous nation-states. And the ongoing relationship between provincial governments and the federal government gives provincial premiers a chance to dabble in statecraft, diplomacy and the "national interest." In recent years the institution of first ministers' conferences, with a permanent Ottawa secretariat and an agenda ranging from the constitution to the economy to social issues, represents a deliberative level of government that supersedes both the national parliament and provincial legislatures and provides the leaders of each regional fiefdom with frequent opportunities to vividly demonstrate why governing a balkanized nation like Canada is such an absurd task.

Perhaps largely by force of geography, British Columbia, the third largest province, has never played a significant role in the mainstream of national politics, and it is the only mainland province not to have produced a prime minister. W. A. C. Bennett developed a tradition of fighting against the apparent indifference of federal governments to the needs of British Columbia. His relations with Ottawa were usually antagonistic, always controversial.

He often would not attend federal-provincial meetings, earning for British Columbia the sobriquet of "the empty chair" of confederation. When he did attend, he brought with him the smallest delegation of officials—thus criticizing the costliness of such exercises—and he often upstaged the other politicians with his bold and disputatious proposals. Back at home he mastered the art of fending off the federal government and portrayed himself as the protector of British Columbia's rights and the defender of its interests within Canada. He was fond of saying: "British Columbia is three thousand miles from Ottawa, but Ottawa is three *million* miles from British Columbia."

Although Dave Barrett did not serve as premier long enough to have much effect on the province's role in federal-provincial relations, he did continue W. A. C.'s tradition of battling distant Ottawa in a flamboyant, attention-getting fashion. His premiership, coinciding with Pierre Trudeau's tenure as prime minister, was given to highly adversarial relations with Ottawa, with rhetorical flourishes, strong ideological overtones and even episodes of public bad language. If anything, Barrett reinforced British Columbia's image as "the spoilt child of confederation."

Bill Bennett tried to change all of that. He wanted to succeed where his predecessors had failed. As part of his program to professionalize and modernize his government, he became a willing and active participant in the processes of Canadian federalism, and during his first years as premier reduced the tensions with Ottawa so dramatically that pundits in the rest of Canada began to take approving notice of British Columbia's new-found moderation. This prompted W. A. C., in his last years, to caution his son: "They seem to like you in Ottawa. And in Toronto they're writing glowing editorials about you. But what do they think of you in Spuzzum, B.C.?"

Yet Bennett's activist role in national affairs did not in any appreciable manner alter British Columbia's place in confederation. For instance, in 1981 he chaired the provincial premiers during the crucial final stages in the constitutional negotiations, and he engaged in a cross-country exercise in shuttle diplomacy to secure an elusive consensus amongst first ministers. In the end the negotiations successfully resulted in a repatriated constitution and a Canadian charter of rights, but Bill Bennett's role as one of the fathers of reconfederation was not responsible for the constitutional accord. Ironically, it was a home-grown issue that catapulted Bennett onto the national stage. This was the policy of restraint.

Fiscal conservatism was hardly a new tack for Bennett; indeed, the idea of restraint in government spending coincided with the rebirth of Social Credit following the budgetary deficit during the NDP's last year in office. In 1977 Bill Bennett was publicly advocating that governments develop tough spending guidelines and budget on five-year cycles. At a first ministers' conference the next year he formally proposed guidelines that included the suggestion that all government spending be limited to the rate of economic growth minus 1 per cent, and that public sector salaries should follow, not lead, the private sector.

However, Bennett was held back by a lack of will at the national level to address such issues and by a booming provincial economy that supported spending increases in Victoria of a billion dollars per year. In fact, the continued growth of government in British Columbia seemed inexorable until a faltering economy during his second term woke Bennett up to the challenge of alerting his government and his province to the need for restraint. It was in this economic challenge that Bill Bennett would find his mission.

The premier could not sell his tough message alone. In the fall of 1981, as the economic situation was rapidly deteriorating, Patrick Kinsella assumed the sensitive position of deputy minister to the premier. Kinsella was forced to deal with strong local biases against "experts"—especially those from eastern Canada, unfamiliar with the nuances of B.C. politics. He was closely scrutinized by the media, by the opposition and by the Socreds as well, for they too were highly skeptical of his purported ability to contribute to their political goals. In Kinsella's view:

> I never set out to endear myself to the media when I arrived. I wanted to low-ball my participation. That was an agreement that Bill Bennett and I had—that I should not be seen nor heard, because he was running a big enough risk having a political hack out here running his office. So the media decided that I was the enemy. I never talked to them—I never had any time for them. I came out here and on the first day I was influential and instrumental in what Bill Bennett said and did. And the media resented that. I came out here as the instant expert on how Bill Bennett should walk and talk.

Kinsella's introduction to west coast politics, on the occasion of the speech from the throne in November 1981, was hardly "lowball." During the ensuing debate on the speech, one NDP member was so argumentative that Kinsella, seated in the chamber for the special occasion, told him to shut up. The premier was forced to apologize for "conduct not becoming a member of my staff." Kinsella thereby received a harsh lesson in the protocol between elected representatives—even opposition MLAs—and nonelected officials in British Columbia. A short time later it was revealed that Kinsella had ordered $15,000 worth of furniture for his new office. The embarrassed premier was forced once again to intervene, and the furniture order was cancelled.

Bennett must have wondered then about the wisdom of recruiting Kinsella, but he recognized his adviser's key role in the political battle ahead. So with a small reorganization at the senior level in his office, Bill Bennett would discover a satisfactory division of labour between the two important dimensions of his mandate: leading a political party and managing a government. And with it, too, he was building a high-powered institution with centralized authority over both the Socred party and the provincial government.

Kinsella was moved to the new post of principal secretary to the premier, where there would be no illusion about the political nature of his duties. The deputy minister's role was filled by Norman Spector, a bright, young academic also from Ontario, who would co-ordinate policy for the duration of Bennett's premiership. Until this time Bennett did not have many independent sources of advice in government; he was, in Spector's words, "rather naked." He had relied to a limited extent on a few senior deputy ministers such as Jim Matkin in Intergovernmental Affairs and Larry Bell in Finance. But for these officials, dealing directly with the premier, rather than through their own ministers, could be awkward, and the few other individuals who had frequent contact with Bennett were inappropriate advisers. As a result, Bennett had been suffering from a kind of intellectual malnutrition that visits leaders surrounded by yes-men who do not tell the truth. According to cabinet minister Garde Gardom:

One didn't find tough advice in an office run by people who had

never been elected. Too many yes-men and spoon-feeding. There
was a lot of resentment about that, particularly from ministers who
might not have as much resolve as others. People became so gun-
shy that they were afraid to cross the street without getting an okay
from somebody. A cabinet minister is intellectually finished under
those circumstances. And there was evidence of that towards the
end.

For this reason, the position of Norman Spector as deputy minister was so important. Many cabinet ministers resented Spector's
influence with Bennett. The B.C. populist tradition, Spector believed, has created a particularly acute tension between public servants and ministers:

> For the premier to be seen to be setting up his own independent
> source of advice was not the thing to be doing. The real issue was
> not between public servants and politicians, it was between the pre-
> mier and his ministers. I think the basic question was whether the
> premier would be in a position to impose his vision on the cor-
> poration—on the government—or whether the division managers
> would be setting the agenda. Obviously in most organizations there
> is a fine balance, but generally the CEO will provide a vision for
> the corporation and, secondly, will maintain a handle on a number
> of issues that are vital to the organization's survival and progress.

Spector was a source of strength for the premier as he developed
his vision of restraint and the means by which that vision would be
implemented. The unlikely duo of businessman and academic de-
vised policies and programs that would radically alter public
administration in British Columbia, a goal to be achieved in a
highly centralized fashion, using government resources in a co-
ordinated manner, and without building up a large bureaucracy in
the premier's office, which remained very lean by any standard.

The government's first, modest restraint program was proclaimed by the Ministry of Finance in August 1981, in the same
week that Norman Spector joined the premier's office. Finance
Minister Hugh Curtis announced that the program, which included a hiring freeze on civil servants, cutbacks on spending, and
higher charges for some government services, was intended to help
avoid a budget deficit at the end of the 1981–82 fiscal year. Later

in 1981, as the economy continued to nosedive, a halt was placed on all government capital projects. The government was hesitant to use the word *recession*, but economic conditions were evidently changing for the worse in a way never before experienced: high inflation, high unemployment, plummeting government revenues, growing expenditures. The resource-based B.C. economy was particularly vulnerable to these uncontrollable forces as the economic pendulum swung back from the heady rise of British Columbia. Just as W. A. C. Bennett had presided over the industrialization of the province, now his son would govern during its "deindustrialization."

At a cabinet retreat at Nanoose Bay in January of 1982 David Emerson, then a finance official, delivered one of the most important presentations ever made to a B.C. cabinet. Emerson, who was helping Bennett set the stage for a serious re-evaluation of all government spending, held that in small, open economies like British Columbia's there were leakages:

> You spend a dollar in B.C. and that dollar doesn't stay in B.C.—it leaks out very, very quickly. And so you can't have a very big effect on the level of demand in the economy by spending domestically. The way the demand is affected is by external forces, more specifically resource markets. And so we developed our thinking about the economy as one essentially driven by natural resource markets, meaning commodity prices in the world marketplace.

Natural resource prices were strong throughout the 1970s, and the supply side was booming with new mines, new mills and new oil and gas fields. In 1980 the Socred administration noticed that inflation was running ahead of increases in commodity prices, which meant real resource prices were declining. Emerson, who would later serve as Bennett's deputy minister of finance, conjectured that the B.C. economy was going into a period of structural decline.

> The first talk of a recession coming, publicly, must have been around January or February 1982. There was a little bit of talk among forecasters that we might see a slight downturn or a slowdown in rates of growth. There wasn't a soul out there who was predicting we would have the worst recession since the depression.

How do you run a government fiscally when your whole economy is driven by natural resource markets? The options were extremely limited. Seeing that the economy was going into a downturn, you could not, in fact *should not,* turn around and deficit spend in order to get yourself out of it, because all that would do would be to dig a deeper hole.

The only way you can affect the fundamentals is by supply-side measures, cost-side measures, because we're essentially selling into a world marketplace, the demand of which we cannot affect. The only thing we can do is affect our market share, and the main way we can do that is through our costs, which means productivity, government costs, taxes, wages—that whole supply-side nexus.

So my urgings were for the government to deal with the cost-side problem. And that was going to hurt.

Some cabinet ministers believed that "Dr. Doom" was simply an alarmist. Premier Bennett, however, agreed with both the diagnosis and the prescription. Soon after, he travelled to Ottawa for a first ministers' conference on the economy at which he railed against the Trudeau administration's policy of high interest rates and urged the assembled leaders to commit themselves to "controlling government spending at all levels." Two weeks later, in a province-wide television broadcast on 18 February, Bennett announced his Restraint on Government program: growth in government spending would generally be limited to 12 per cent, while a Compensation Stabilization Program (CSP) would hold salary increases in the public sector to 10 per cent, plus or minus 2 per cent for flexibility and inflation and an additional 2 per cent for productivity—thus public servants were provided with potential increases between 8 and 14 per cent. A commissioner would be appointed to administer the program and to interpret, enforce and revise these guidelines as necessary. His rulings would be final and binding.

Even though Bennett considered his restraint program only "a gentle application of the brakes," it was the focus of much criticism; in particular, the B.C. Government Employees' Union (BCGEU) and other public sector unions lambasted the CSP for its threat to collective bargaining rights. But as the economy worsened, the Socred government was forced to hit the brakes harder, and then harder yet. In fact, later in 1982, confronted with an unprecedented and unavoidable deficit, Bennett ordered a select group of deputy ministers to put together a plan to slash up to 25 per cent of public sector employees from the province's payroll.

Politics clearly was not a consideration in Bennett's determined pursuit of restraint. The public opinion research available to the premier indicated that a government deficit was not high on the list of public concerns. In a country of economic illiterates, the premier's new political advisers found it easy to counsel him to forget restraint, forget the deficit, for these simply were not political issues. Yet Bill Bennett was unremitting in his wish to go forward. But in order to go forward, he recognized the need to obtain a decisive electoral mandate.

Almost from the time the ballots had been counted for the Socreds' narrow 1979 victory, there were rumours of snap elections in the B.C. air. The combination of political and economic instability during those hectic years produced a frenzied, nervous atmosphere. The news media was prone to wild rumour-mongering, but the opposition, still under the leadership of Dave Barrett, was strangely quiescent. Apparently their strategy was to simply bide their time and allow the government to self-destruct by means of a seemingly deadly combination of political scandals and economic crises.

But the NDP had ample opportunity to learn that Bill Bennett's Socreds were easily underestimated. Most important was the Kamloops by-election of May 1981, a contest that virtually all observers conceded to the opposition. Indeed the Socreds, by their own polling, entered the by-election nineteen points behind the NDP. This was the first electoral skirmish to use some of the political techniques Hugh Harris had brought to British Columbia, and they proved successful—Socred Claude Richmond was narrowly elected. The victory temporarily bolstered Bennett's flagging leadership and also seemed to vindicate his efforts to build a new party organization that used modern campaign methods.

Bennett's cabinet shuffle in August 1982 seemed designed to help brace his administration for tough times ahead. He moved senior members of his cabinet—hard-liners—into those portfolios that would bear the brunt of criticism towards the restraint program, prompting the Vancouver *Province* to suggest that Bennett's pretensions "to moderation, flexibility and the middle-of-the-road" were now gone.

The cabinet was split over a fall 1982 election, but the political professionals were poised for the premier to drop the election writ. Armed with favourable polls and a revved-up election machine, they attempted to persuade him to go. But Bennett felt the party had peaked and had no momentum. He believed the government's difficult programs were only just beginning to be felt. And he feared the opposition would run a fear campaign. He told the cabinet that the public needed more time to understand the severity of the recession, and once they did, and once they recognized that the government was facing it, they would support Social Credit.

Bennett put a halt to election preparations in September at a meeting attended by his key advisers, including Patrick Kinsella, Jerry Lampert (who had become the party's executive director after Hugh Harris's death in April), Allan Gregg, Nancy McLean and a young political organizer who had helped with the important Kamloops by-election, Bud Smith. They were disappointed with the premier's decision, but it was his alone to take. And Bennett's acquired sense of political timing was borne out by future polls which showed that the Socreds' popularity had in fact peaked in September and dropped sharply immediately thereafter. An election at that time would have been disastrous for the party. In the spring of 1983, however, as the polls began to show another increase in support, Bennett sensed a gathering momentum that would allow him to announce the long-awaited election for 5 May.

The 1983 election was a crucial battle in the history of political warfare in British Columbia. Going into the contest, Bennett had an opportunity to do both some team building and house cleaning. Attorney General Allan Williams had already announced his resignation from politics. And in a surprise move Bill Vander Zalm, who had been shuffled from Municipal Affairs and within a short while had become extremely controversial in the Education portfolio, also announced his departure.

Vander Zalm's declaration that he might be back one day met with a great deal of skepticism. The Vancouver *Province* said of the insurgent politician's exit: "The only sure thing is that Bill Vander Zalm will not fade quietly from the political scene. When (and if) he departs permanently, it will be not with a whimper, but with a bang."

In the 1983 campaign there were also Bennett loyalists who

would like to have retired from politics, but their leader's sense of duty and commitment compelled them to stay. Finance Minister Hugh Curtis said:

> I did not want to run again in '83. My wife and I had talked about it. I went to the premier very close to the election call and said: "It's been great, and I don't want to do it again." And that was probably the sharpest argument we ever had, because he said: "You have to run again. That's the end of the conversation. You have to run again. The minister of finance in this province can't leave in the midst of a recession." And he didn't dismiss me, but the rest of it was just my spouting and saying: "Well I'd like to leave."
> "Well you can't."
> "Well what else can we talk about?"
> Obviously he had looked at the same problem from his own perspective. The premier can't leave in the midst of a recession. If he said that I couldn't, then obviously he had said to himself: "I can't."

Bennett knew that the government's re-election was not assured—in fact an NDP victory was widely predicted—but he wanted to make the campaign one of issues. His father's administration had been defeated in 1972 while advocating the first formal restraint program initiated by a Canadian government. W. A. C. had proposed that public service salary increases be limited to 6.5 per cent to protect against the onset of inflation. But the premier's warnings about inflation and the need to contain government costs fell upon deaf ears. During the election campaign civil servants and teachers rebelled against this policy and successfully campaigned against the government. Now Bill Bennett was determined to win on the same issue, making it, if need be, his last stand as well. In his view,

> the public did not have in their mind that we were in a recession. It hadn't filtered down to them yet. But the government was in difficulty. We were going into a changed economy. Therefore, we had to sell the message. But we found out the public didn't understand the word *restraint*—they weren't in favour of what we had to do. Only 15 per cent or so had any idea and appreciated it. We started from that difficult position.

The Social Credit Party centred its campaign on restraint, although the government had several "bold, new initiatives" to speak of, including Vancouver's B.C. Place development, boasting Canada's first covered stadium; plans for Expo 86, which had been officially proclaimed by Queen Elizabeth at a ceremony in the new stadium; Vancouver's advanced light rapid transit system, the first of its kind in the world; plans to construct the Coquihalla highway to the interior of the province; and the massive northeast coal development, which was beginning production in 1983. These "megaprojects," funded with billions of dollars of public and private investment, had been on the drawing board for years and were now coming to fruition when the sluggish B.C. economy would benefit greatly from the job creation and construction activity associated with them. However, the Socreds' campaign did not so much focus on these important projects as it did on the need for a cautious approach to economic issues and restraint in further government spending. It was probably the first election campaign in Canada in which a governing party was promising less, not more.

The NDP were running ahead of the Socreds as the campaign commenced, but it was a close race. The 1979 results had shown how government could be won by only a relatively few votes in key constituencies. Dave Barrett was squaring off for one final grudge match with Bennett, to be played with all the classic themes of B.C. politics: personality, paranoia, polarization and populism. Barrett was presented in his pin-striped election attire, trying to look premieral, his handlers attempting to keep him as quiet and low-key as possible. In direct contrast to the Social Credit campaign, which stressed neoconservative solutions to the province's ailing economy, the opposition party proposed to borrow up to half a billion dollars to create jobs in a 1980s version of a Depression-era New Deal program. But the New Democrats were hoping less for an NDP victory than for a Social Credit defeat.

With the Social Credit Party's fresh organization and highly charged political machine, the foibles and follies of past campaigns were mostly absent from the Socred effort of '83, but whether or not an expensive, professional organization would make a difference was as yet unclear.

Serving as Bennett's campaign tour director was Bud Smith, a young but experienced political campaigner with strong roots in the federal Progressive Conservative Party. The B.C.-born Smith was a lawyer by training, had an almost encyclopaedic knowledge of British Columbia and communicated freely and easily with the premier. Smith also held a different view of the premier's combative style, believing that rather than attempt to modify that image, in politics "you take the victim as you find him."

Dave Barrett's campaign meetings were loud, noisy, cheerful affairs, while the premier's were quiet, intense, almost sombre at times. Commentators concluded that this was strong evidence of a pending NDP victory. In Bud Smith's view:

> It was a matter of selling a message. The '83 campaign was very much a campaign of issues, profound issues. And they were discussed continuously throughout the campaign in the context of the future of British Columbia. It is not an easy thing to do, to go out and sell people the notion that they are going to have to take less. This is something that almost every politician is told never to try. Premier Bennett frankly didn't deviate very much from his game plan. People were listening to what was being said—they were understanding the dimension of the problem that was being addressed. Whereas with Barrett, they were being entertained.

Election campaigns are emotional roller coasters. Each day is filled with surprises while efforts are made to ride along with the ever-changing moods of campaign organizations, the media and, of course, the electorate. The events of one day—14 April, the premier's birthday—illustrate what can go wrong in even the best-organized campaign.

Well before sunrise Bennett and his team—including Bud Smith and executive assistant Mike Bailey—flew from Kelowna to Terrace, arriving behind schedule. The premier was rushed to a radio station for a live interview but ran into a noisy, well-organized demonstration and was pelted with eggs and tomatoes. Bud Smith recognized in the "local" crowd of demonstrators many of the same faces that he had seen at similar events during the previous few days. From Terrace, Bennett flew to Stewart, on the Alaska border, for a swing through the Atlin constituency. There was a good turnout in the small town, and Bennett also visited the set of the Hollywood movie *Iceman*.

After flying back to Terrace to rejoin his campaign entourage, the premier travelled by bus to Smithers where an evening speech was scheduled. Bennett, who was suffering from the flu, retired to a hotel room, giving express orders that he was not to be disturbed. Meanwhile his handlers had discovered from the party advance-man in the constituency that the local candidate's campaign advertisements contained embarrassing factual errors and that another demonstration was to be expected at the evening function. When Bailey and Bud Smith went to collect their leader and tell him the news, they found a distraught and emotional premier. As Bailey recalled:

> We knocked on his room and he said: "Bailey, I've had seven phone calls put through to this room!" We could see he was not in a tremendous mood. We told him about the local issues, and I remember he just flew off the handle. He threw his pen at the wall. He said: "Why the hell are you telling me this now? Don't you know I've got to go make a speech?" It was not a fun time. It was just the maddest I've ever seen him.

Although no protest materialized that evening, an incident did occur that could have been disastrous for Bennett's campaign. In spite of his exhaustion, Bennett was delivering an effective speech, but was interrupted now and then by a heckler whose comments grew louder and louder. Eventually the man, a native Indian, said he was thirsty, wanted a drink and needed some money. Bennett reached into his pocket and withdrew a twenty-dollar bill, which he handed to the man.

The incident had all the makings of a major racial slur. Following the speech, however, Bud Smith boarded the media bus and worked the reporters to ensure the incident would not be blown out of proportion. The premier was himself despondent over what had happened, and as he flew back to Vancouver late that night he muttered to a couple of reporters: "This has been the worst day of my life." That worst day ended at Vancouver airport, beyond two o'clock in the morning, twenty-two hours after it began.

The events of the premier's birthday contrast those of one week later, 21 April, as the Socred and NDP leaders campaigned in the province's southeast corner. On that day, Barrett stated that an NDP administration would scrap the Compensation Stabilization Program, implying that he was not committed to the principle of or need for restraint. While NDP strategists and party workers groaned at their leader's gaffe, the news media scrambled to make it the lead story of the day. The media travelling with Premier Bennett wanted a quick response.

Bud Smith and Pat Kinsella, after determining the significance of Barrett's mistake, allowed a TV crew into Bennett's Cranbrook hotel room for a live feed on the six o'clock news. With only minutes to go before the broadcast, the premier was awakened from a much-needed nap and briefed. Kinsella, especially excited about what he saw as the magnitude of Barrett's error, explained the crucial nature of the moment to a groggy Bennett, who was dressing and shaving and listening all at once. The premier said to Smith and Kinsella: "I don't understand why you fellows think this is such a big deal. Barrett's said that dozens of times before. He's said it in the House. That's not news."

With only seconds to spare, the premier was seated in front of the camera—special attention was paid to the camera angle, as Bennett was not fully dressed—and at precisely six o'clock BCTV's news anchor, Tony Parsons, introduced the lead story. Viewers throughout the province then saw Bennett calmly, slowly indicate deep regret that the opposition leader did not believe in the need for restraint. It was a smooth, convincing performance. Kinsella, Smith and other key Socred strategists were elated. They now felt the election was in the bag. For the remainder of the campaign the Socreds kept a relatively low profile, while the NDP attempted to qualify or clarify their leader's indiscretion.

Many observers believed that Barrett's rejection of the need for government restraint altered the tone and dynamics of the election and marked a turning point in the campaign. But this was also disputed by many, including Bud Smith, who thought that Barrett's comment simply reminded people of the days of the NDP administration. "The drama of the moment firmed up the decision that the people were already taking," said Smith.

Bennett was very much aware that the re-election of his government rested heavily on his shoulders. One error—real or imagined —could have devastating consequences for the party. Bennett keenly felt that responsibility to his party and to the thousands of volunteers, workers, fund raisers and voters who were relying on him to win. The day before the election Bennett, Smith, Kinsella and Mike Bailey were having lunch at a restaurant on Vancouver Island. Smith recalled:

A fellow who was sitting there—it could have been a tourist, it could have been anyone—got up to pay his bill. And he walks by Premier Bennett and puts his hand on his shoulder and he says simply: "You better goddamned well win tomorrow." And he had a demeanour about him that you couldn't help but think that he indeed meant what he was saying. It really rocked the premier. It brought home that sense of responsibility one more time.

In the end Bennett's Socreds did win, surprising most pundits by electing thirty-five MLAs to the NDP's twenty-two. The Socreds received almost 50 per cent of the vote, while the NDP received the support of 45 per cent. Third parties were again shut out. The election clearly represented a strong personal victory for Bill Bennett. There was no question that he could and would take complete credit for his government's re-election. And immediately he set to work defining his new mandate.

During the campaign—when decision making in government came to a virtual halt—Norman Spector had been preparing the transitional material for the winner. The material included detailed descriptions of the organization of each government ministry, the requirements of each minister (or the "burden of the office") and a summary of thirty-day issues, sixty-day issues and one-year issues affecting the government. These transition documents fit into three six-inch-thick binders. The morning after the election Spector flew to Kelowna, taking these materials to his boss:

The premier said: "Well, that's all fine. Now, here's what we have to do." And he set out about ten things. "Here's what we're going to do. Here's what I want to accomplish in this term. And we'll be holding a cabinet retreat within a few weeks. So you get the deputies to take all of this material and repackage it with these objectives and goals in mind."

Bill Bennett clearly knew what he wanted to do and how he wanted to do it. Shortly after the election victory, his new cabinet and their deputies put together the details of the next dramatic stage in British Columbia's restraint revolution. At a cabinet retreat at a resort on Okanagan Lake, the premier energetically threw himself into the task of leading, directing and prodding his team towards a firm consensus on the strong measures needed to address the province's economic woes. Bennett felt far more secure in his leadership than ever before, and, significantly, for the first time his new cabinet was without a deputy premier. Bennett unceremoniously stripped this title from Grace McCarthy, who remained as minister of human resources. It had taken him several years, but the premier was about to become a premier. Bennett later said:

> Everyone knew the task that had to be done. Everyone was offering up suggestions on what programs should be eliminated and how we could reduce costs. I had to reinforce that it was as tough as the Finance Ministry's forecasts said it was. The forecasts were getting worse, and we had to get costs under control.
>
> And we had enthusiasm for the task. It was like religion. It was a zeal that we were going to be martyrs to do the right thing.

The "task" was still restraint, but a serious and more determined brand than had been seen before. Bennett invited Michael Walker, head of the right-wing economic think-tank, the Fraser Institute, to talk to the cabinet to help set the tone for the government's concerted drive towards restraint. Although Bennett was clearly the architect of restraint in British Columbia, critics of the Social Credit administration suggested, incorrectly, that the program was the brainchild of Walker and the Fraser Institute. Others suggested that perhaps senior bureaucrats such as Norman Spector had fathered the program. Spector said of the distinction between policy formulation and implementation:

> Some of the specifics were the premier's, some were his ministers'. Ministers would say "Here's my proposal" and "Here's my proposal"—and some were accepted and some were not. The officials played an important part, but it's also worth observing that part of the populism of British Columbia, both before '83 and after, is that ministers play a much more active role in the implementation and design of policy than they do elsewhere in the country. The formulation of the policy was at the political level, with advice from bureaucrats.

For Premier Bennett it was absolutely crucial to the success of the program for cabinet ministers and their senior officials to be solidly united behind the government's goals and to push forward the implementation of restraint as soon as possible. The government had gone into the 1983 election without introducing a budget for the new fiscal year; therefore a summer session of the legislature was on the agenda to approve both a new budget and legislation. On 7 July Finance Minister Hugh Curtis presented the budget, which revealed an unprecedented deficit of more than $1.6 billion. That by itself sounded alarm bells in the legislative chamber. But it was nothing compared with the clamour that followed the immediate introduction of twenty-seven bills that represented a far-reaching, radical program to substantially decrease the cost and size of government in British Columbia.

The most controversial proposals included restrictions to the ambit of collective bargaining in the public sector, provisions for the dismissal of government employees without cause, elimination of the office of the rentalsman, increased powers for the minister of education over schools and other educational institutions, an indefinite extension of the government's Compensation Stabilization Program, scrapping the legislature's Crown Corporations Review Committee, elimination of the provincial motor vehicle inspection system, increased powers conferred on the Medical Services Commission over physicians and surgeons in British Columbia as well as restrictions on the issuance of medical billing numbers, the disbanding of the Employment Standards Board and the replacement of the human rights branch of the Ministry of Labour with the Human Rights Commission. In short, these measures cut existing programs and centralized power in Victoria.

Bennett's restraint package hit the political scene like a thunderbolt, and intense attention was focussed on the Social Credit government. For three months the House debated the legislation and argued over the need for such extreme measures. Provincial and national news media concentrated attention on Bill Bennett, curious as never before about the man behind the restraint revolution. Meanwhile, a wide coalition of dissent built among diverse special interest groups. The protests quickly came together under the banner of Operation Solidarity—perhaps the most formidable extraparliamentary opposition to a freely elected government ever seen in Canada.

Bennett explained to the legislature: "When you get a 60 per cent drop in resource revenues and a drop in the economy, obviously government has to restrain its budget, constrain its costs and set priorities. That's what being government is all about— making tough choices." However, most observers believed that the restraint package was motivated as much by ideology as by economics. The storms of protest were a reaction not only to cuts in programs and services but also to the government's blitzkrieg approach to restraint and to the political nature of some elements of the package.

Norman Spector later steadfastly refused to either defend or question government policy, although he did say that "there was a well-articulated vision and understanding of the economy." On the strategy of surprising the legislature with all the bills on the same day, Bennett later said:

> I think there were a couple of bills there that shouldn't have been included, because they were for another reason. The mistake was in trying to clean up the human rights branch into the new committee —it shouldn't have been done at the same time, because what it did was confuse it. It blended in a strong philosophical campaign. And it broadened the alliance against us.
>
> Amongst my colleagues, many will say that we shouldn't have put all the bills in at once. But we worked on them and agreed that everything that was ready would go in. I take full responsibility for that. I'll justify it. I believe that you put it all in—you lay out the extent of the program, rather than dribble it in. And you give the people a chance to see what's coming down. Because you're not going to pass all those bills in one day or ten days—it's going to take months. And I believe that you only take the fight once. Others said: "You should dribble them in and fight them off one at a time." I said: "They'll kill us bit by bit. They'll make us start to back up. Our members would become afraid at some point to do the whole program. But put it out there, and we'll circle our wagons and fight together if that's what it takes."
>
> The whole caucus stood solid during the opposition—there were no breaks in cabinet or caucus. I think if we had dribbled them in, the program would have had trouble. You'd do what most governments do, you'd say, "Who needs this? If the public doesn't want this, why are we doing it?" I had some of that, but our people all stayed.

Some critics suggested that Bill Bennett had somehow tricked the electorate, that he had no mandate to do what he was doing. In fact, those critics were denouncing a consistent politician who had the audacity to do what he had promised. To other observers restraint demonstrated a kind of schizophrenia on the part of the Socreds, in that they were dismantling programs they had themselves initiated. Another way of looking at that would be to say it was the ultimate demonstration of political responsiveness. Even though they were originally Social Credit policies and programs, the government could no longer afford to be married to them. Nevertheless, there is some validity to the criticism that restraint had a political dimension. Deputy Minister of Finance David Emerson later said:

> I think it is fair to say that part of the commitment people had to restraint was because they viewed it as an opportunity. If they had to do things over again, there were a lot of things that they wouldn't have put into place, a lot of programs, special offices and so on. I think that's the same with any government. I think they started to see restraint as a tool to get rid of things that they had always wanted to get rid of. So to some degree the political calculation that went into some of those cuts was a bad one in that the cut itself wasn't worth the political noise. In some cases, people have argued that it wasn't a saving at all and in fact resulted in cost increases and was just a political agenda. And I think you're going to get that in any tough program. You're going to have some horror stories. A lot of those cuts were not the sort of things a fiscal adviser would recommend.

While the NDP fought in the legislature, Operation Solidarity, backed by the B.C. labour movement, fought in the streets. On 23 July approximately twenty thousand people protested in front of Vancouver's B.C. Place stadium. The next week more than twenty-five thousand angry demonstrators converged on the lawns of the legislature in Victoria to hear fiery speeches from union leaders, human rights activists and clergymen. On 10 August a monster rally at Empire Stadium attracted as many as fifty thousand people. And in Vancouver on 15 October, coinciding with the Social Credit Party's annual convention, perhaps the largest political demonstration ever in British Columbia—as many as sixty thousand marchers—took to the streets.

All during these demonstrations, throughout the summer and into the fall, the legislature sat, day after day, night after night, filibuster after filibuster, putting the pieces of the restraint package into the province's statute books. It soon became clear that most of the bills would pass, but that legislation affecting the relationship between public sector employees and their employers would be the focus for the final stand of both the official and unofficial opposition forces. Operation Solidarity spoke bravely of a general strike, and opinion polls showed that, while the public endorsed the government's objectives, they were unhappy about the methods used to implement restraint.

David Emerson did not think organized protests and threats of civil disobedience had any effect on the fundamentals of the package; rather they probably "steeled Bennett's resolve" to the program. "If you were going to challenge him to a gunfight on main street, he wasn't going to back down. And I think that's what a lot of it was—it was a gunfight on main street." Bennett himself said at the time: "This province will never be run by demonstrators and protestors as long as we're government."

Norman Spector remembered that there was a lot of second guessing, especially on the part of those who had been responsible for some of the measures in the package. "The premier's view was that any backing down would simply whet the appetite of those who wanted to overturn the entire package."

One of the frightening sides of restraint for Bennett—and an example of the kinds of pressures borne by a leader—were the threats of violence against him and his family. At his son Brad's wedding in the summer of 1983, he shook hands with about five undercover policemen he had not known were present. "I thought they were friends of the bride."

The compounding effect of the huge protest rallies, the rancorous legislative opposition, the melodramatic media and the personal death threats produced in the premier a personal and political revelation, significantly changing the way he viewed the consequences of leadership.

If politicians have any fear at all, I became the least afraid in my whole life in political terms. I was not fearful of losing. There was an awareness that this is what politics is all about. What I was doing was right, and people would understand, and I would not be doing the province a favour by backing down.

What I learned was to handle what most politicians fear: opposition so great that you fear the political cost, or the physical cost, or anything else. That's the only major change I ever had. The rest was the cumulative, gradual effect of leadership.

I suddenly became aware that I wasn't afraid of political cost. It was important. If I had known it earlier, I might have been more forceful earlier. Because I was more ready to assess the political cost early in my career than I was in the latter part.

The premier's fearlessness allowed him to play a brave game of brinkmanship. In October, when the opposition to restraint peaked, he adjourned the legislature for a "cooling off period" and shifted attention to the ongoing negotiations between the government and its employees. The province was plunging towards a massive confrontation. The BCGEU went on strike on 1 November, and a week later teachers began walking the picket lines. More talk of a general strike from the B.C. Federation of Labour and Operation Solidarity formed the background to a crucial set of negotiations, which were now directed by Norman Spector. Jack Munro, the blustery, profane regional president of the International Woodworkers of America, the province's largest private sector union, was representing public sector groups in these last-ditch negotiations. As Bill Bennett prepared to celebrate a decade as leader of the Social Credit Party, a dramatic evening meeting took place at his home in Kelowna. The premier, Munro and Spector hammered out the Kelowna Accord, which effectively ended the protests, the opposition and Operation Solidarity. The accord saw the government drop one highly contentious bill and make compromises to some aspects of collective bargaining in the public sector and procedures for reductions in the public service. But the bulk of the restraint program proceeded as Bennett had intended. There was not much backing down on main street.

The major crisis was over, but the discord and tensions within British Columbia would last for a long time. Operation Solidarity, lacking strong leadership, faded away in bitterness, never able to emerge as a positive or constructive force. Jack Munro was blamed by public sector unionists and others for a "sell out" with the Kelowna Accord, but in his own pragmatic way Munro realized that the protest could not, as some had hoped, go on forever. Said Munro:

The Bennett government created the climate to put together a whole raft of groups of people who never, ever really had the ability to get together before. These groups of people all of a sudden find this fantastic power where people are talking strikes in the public sector and general strikes in the private sector and all this. . . . They thought this is fuckin' great. The same people who had never ever in their goddamned life . . . thought they would sit down at an executive board and make these kinds of decisions . . . [were] making a decision to shut the province down. It was great. Trade unionists . . . we were the turkeys in the goddamned thing. Chicken-shit trade unionists. You could feel that we were the goddamned moderates. . . . I should have been for all these causes, a lot of causes that I don't goddamned agree with. I should have been asking our people, who maybe were going into a strike situation of our own, to come off the job. Well that isn't the way the real world works.

Back in the real world the phenomenon of Operation Solidarity had clearly caused a crisis for Dave Barrett and the NDP—a protest movement had usurped the party's role as the official opposition. Compounding this was a lack of leadership. Not long after the 1983 election, Dave Barrett announced his resignation. The NDP provincial council decided against a quick leadership convention and would wait until May 1984 to choose a new leader. As a result, the legislative opposition was virtually leaderless while the restraint program was pushed through the legislature. One of Dave Barrett's last hurrahs occurred in the early hours of the morning on 6 October 1983 during an all-night sitting of the legislature, after closure had been invoked to ensure passage of key elements of the restraint program. Challenging a ruling from the chair, Barrett, in his belligerent fashion, carried on out of order until he had to be dragged from the House, unceremoniously dumped in the corridor and banished from the legislature until the end of the session. A pathetic conclusion to a remarkable career.

Dave Barrett will be remembered as British Columbia's first NDP premier—and that memory will be coloured by controversy and confrontation. His flamboyant skills as an orator, his incompetence as an administrator and his intensely martial personality poisoned politics in the province and seriously divided his party. With his acerbic tongue and quick one-liners, he developed a reputation as a kind of clown prince of politics, producing smiles

and laughter but not trust. One of his colleagues, who had served
in the short-lived NDP cabinet, was later haunted by Barrett's contradictions: "No one has ever seen past his eyes. Watch him smile.
His eyes don't. He's always talking about sharing and caring, but
he doesn't share or care."

The NDP's failure in the 1975, 1979 and 1983 B.C. elections was
not a signal of the failure of socialism. Indeed, the New Democrats
possessed both the organization and the popular support to win
each of those contests. But in a polarized province where the
politics of personality has grown into a dominating force, leadership and the perceived competence of the party leader tilt the
scales. Dave Barrett's entire career in provincial politics was spent
fighting against the Bennetts. He won once, but then he lost, and
kept on losing. In the field of winners and losers, history will judge
Dave Barrett a loser.

The race to choose a new NDP leader, culminating in the May
1984 leadership convention, revealed much about the socialist
party's style and make-up. The two acknowledged front runners
were Bill King, a former NDP MLA and cabinet minister who represented the party's old guard and allied interest groups, and David
Vickers, a prominent Victoria lawyer and former deputy attorney
general, presenting a fresh new face and a voice of moderation.
The Socreds most feared the election of Vickers, an articulate and
attractive candidate who would undoubtedly have moved the NDP
closer to the centre of the ideological spectrum.

Vickers was comfortably in the lead early in the convention, and
his organization was confident that a final ballot pitting King
against their candidate would produce a Vickers victory. Their concern was that if King lost momentum, some of the lesser candidates might join forces with him to defeat Vickers, a newcomer to
the NDP. One Vickers delegation pushed hard for a strategic move
on the penultimate ballot that would have had enough of their own
delegates vote for King to ensure a final ballot square-off between
the two candidates. They feared that if third-place Bob Skelly, a
relatively unknown MLA, jumped ahead of King, it would produce
the elements of a Stop Vickers movement. The Vickers campaign
committee, after serious consideration, rejected such a move as being too manipulative and potentially too divisive for their party.

As predicted, Skelly squeaked past King, with Vickers still in
the lead. King then locked arms with Skelly and marched around

the convention hall, sending out the word to all of his delegates to "vote for the true socialist." The coalition of established forces in the NDP, particularly organized labour, turned towards Skelly rather than support Vickers, whose socialist credentials were unproven. On the fifth and final ballot, Bob Skelly became the new leader of a bitter and divided party.

By electing a leader who was both strongly ideological and nervous in public, the NDP had certainly not paid much attention to political pragmatism. After the final ballot, disappointed delegates and observers poured from the hall, leaving only half the audience to listen to Skelly's halting acceptance speech. Graham Lea, whose own bid for the party's leadership had been overwhelmingly rejected, stood on the stage with other unsuccessful candidates and outgoing leader Dave Barrett as the new leader groped for words. Lea recalled: "Barrett leaned over to me and said, 'My God, he'll need all the help he can get.' I thought to myself, 'Not from me.'" Shortly thereafter Graham Lea left the NDP to experiment with political independence and the challenge of organizing a third force in B.C. politics. Dave Barrett resigned his seat in the legislature and accepted a job as a Vancouver radio hotline host. And within the B.C. New Democratic Party the prospect of leadership conventions and the joys of democracy would not be welcome for a long time.

Bill Bennett and the Socreds were pleased with the election of Bob Skelly, believing that their biggest challenge would be to not completely underestimate him. The government, taking advantage of the NDP's disarray during this period, continued with its tough political agenda. The ambitious goals of the restraint program were being achieved: wage controls in the public sector were uncompromising; the civil service was reduced by 25 per cent; in 1984 most government ministries spent even less than in the previous year. Although most of the program's objectives were achieved quickly, Bennett would fight a prolonged battle to cut back on increases in social spending and would struggle to contain the costs of education. This resulted in constant public hostility through 1984 and 1985, with the unprecedented firing of elected school boards and the resignation of the president of the University of British Columbia, George Pedersen.

As these battles raged on, the public seemed to grow numb to the pressures that had provoked tough government action. Bill

Bennett acquired the image of a hard, uncaring and dictatorial leader. He preached about the "new reality" of the changing world economy and called those who opposed Socred restraint policies "bad British Columbians"—a local version of an earlier "un-American" phenomenon. Soon the premier's colleagues asked him to stop using the word *restraint*, with its negative associations, and to start focussing attention on some of the government's positive achievements.

The 1985 budget was in part an attempt to refocus the political agenda away from the punishing message of restraint to a more up-beat goal of economic renewal. Bennett even introduced the Critical Industries Commission, appointing former Vancouver mayor and Liberal MP Art Phillips to assist closure-prone resource businesses. Much emphasis was placed on investment in major capital projects. The province's northeast coal development was in operation, generating substantial economic activity in the province's north. (It was argued that this was detrimental to coal producers in the province's southeast and that the new production seriously aggravated a world oversupply of coal.) More positive were the expectations associated with such megaprojects as the Coquihalla highway to the Interior, the Annacis Bridge crossing the Fraser River, and Vancouver's advanced rapid transit system—all scheduled for completion in 1986, Vancouver's centennial and the year of the Vancouver-hosted world's fair.

Most observers felt that Expo 86 would be an important part of Bill Bennett's political itinerary, likely serving as a springboard to another election campaign. But the construction of Expo was plagued with troubles, and it was sometimes questionable whether the world's fair would proceed. In 1981 Bennett had hired Vancouver businessman Jimmy Pattison to serve as his "dollar-a-year" chairman of the board of Expo. Twice Pattison tried to resign, but each time Bennett said: "If I can't count on guys like you who have made a success and made money out of this province, who can I count on?" After some tough cuts to the Expo board's original budget, the premier had little contact with the fair, delegating construction, planning and publicity almost completely to Pattison.

Bennett did interfere once more, in April of 1984. The construction unions had told Pattison that the fair would never be built unless he signed an exclusive agreement with union contractors, thereby shutting out nonunion construction crews. The government's policy was for both union and nonunion workers to work together on the site. The conflict had produced a war of words and even some violent clashes between angry union crews and eager nonunion workers. Pattison said:

> I didn't want the fair to be built and to spend all this money on construction and have a month to go and the thing wasn't finished. We couldn't take the risk. So I said we'd be better off to cancel the fair, unless we had an absolute guarantee that the construction would not be disrupted with strikes and get held up by the labour unions. I was serious. And they gave it to us. They brought in new legislation that would create these special economic zones if we'd apply for them—which we did. Bill Bennett accommodated us.

Bennett's legislative amendment to the Labour Code allowed the cabinet to declare important "economic development projects" as open sites, effectively barring unions from protesting the presence of nonunion workers. Other legislative amendments, combined with the quiet but firm support of the provincial government, ensured that the world's fair proceeded on time and on budget.

Bennett stayed in the background and allowed his handpicked chairman to reap the glory. This thwarted all of the efforts of the premier's advisers, who urged him to accept the acclaim for what was obviously going to be a huge success. In Bill Bennett's refusal there was an important message for his advisers. According to Patrick Kinsella:

> This was an example of his lack of ego. You have a magnificent thing going on in your province like Expo, which is the result of the resolve and determination of Bill Bennett. The untold story of that is that he knew that Pattison had to get credit for it. What other politician in modern times would ever allow that to happen? How many people would have been around Bill Bennett saying: "Premier, you've got to take credit for this. This is the best thing to ever happen in British Columbia. You're going into a pre-election mode . . ."? And yet he stayed away. He knew it was going to be successful. The whole thing was destined to be successful. Not only was it going to be a smash hit, but Bill Bennett could now *safely* take credit for it. There may have been a wariness before because, "Hey, may-

be it isn't going to work, and Jimmy can be the fall guy as well as the hero." But that was never in Bill Bennett's head. He always let Jimmy be the lead guy and throughout it gave him credit. No other politician would ever have done that.

Bill Bennett was never an exuberant, outward-reaching politician, and during this period, as the restraint program was unwinding and as a variety of provincial megaprojects were being completed, he turned inward. No longer afraid of or concerned with "political cost," he retreated into the insularity of his office and the comfort of a few trusted advisers. Following the general election of 1983, Patrick Kinsella left Victoria to join the Sentinel Group, a political-government consulting firm established by Social Credit fund raiser Mike Burns that became a source of deep controversy and bitter wrangling within the party; some long-time members believed that this was a sign of corruption creeping into Social Credit. (Bud Smith had succeeded Kinsella as principal secretary to the premier.)

Bill Bennett's style of leadership during this period is characterized in a meeting that took place in the premier's office in 1984 at the request of Bob Skelly, who wished to discuss some pressing issues related to the forthcoming legislative session. Bennett suggested that Graham Lea, who now sat as an independent MLA, should attend; Bud Smith was also present. As Graham Lea recalled:

> Bennett, at some point, said to Skelly: "I know that things have not always worked well in the past, but I'm telling you that whatever my House leader tells you he will deliver, I will guarantee you I will deliver. Can you guarantee me the same?"
>
> Skelly says: "Well things don't really quite work that way in the NDP caucus—as Graham will tell you. The leader just can't tell people what to do. It's more democratic."
>
> Bennett says: "I'm not here to discuss your problems with democracy. I'm telling you that when my House leader says he will deliver, I will guarantee he will deliver. Can you guarantee me the same?"
>
> And Skelly by this time is twitching and shaking, and he says: "Well not really."
>
> Bennett says: "You know, your problem is you have to decide

whether you're going to be the leader of the caucus or whether you're going to follow that caucus."

Bill Bennett had come a long way from his own tentative, often nervous, first years as a political leader. Although he would always have a difficult public image—one exacerbated by the toughness of the restraint program—there was no question about his leadership over the government or the Social Credit Party. However, with his increasingly centralized power, and isolated within his office, a subtle but intense antagonism grew. Within government circles the "premier's office" became the target of quiet abuse and frustration. Bud Smith said:

> There's a certain mystery about that office. I think that there can be a cult of personality that develops around people in that office. And the premier's office was an "excuse vehicle" or a "blame vehicle" for ministers who couldn't get approval for half-baked or unsellable ideas. "I couldn't get it past the premier's office," they would say.

For Bennett, the proper functioning of his office necessarily bred resentment. He made it clear to all his ministers that their deputy ministers belonged to the government and in executing policy they were accountable to the premier. In a functional sense, this meant that Bennett's deputy, Norman Spector, wielded tremendous power, for he was responsible for co-ordination of all policy as well as carrying some difficult messages to ministers and their bureaucrats. It was almost impossible for some cabinet ministers to accept that these messages had the authority and blessing of the premier. Increasingly, for his colleagues, when Bill Bennett was good, he was very good, and when he was bad, he was Norman Spector. Spector became the scapegoat for all perceived problems in government, a villain who had the ear of the premier. ("The messenger is always in that position," he said. "That's one of the reasons you don't make a career out of those sorts of jobs.") The truth is that Spector's influence was usually exaggerated; the premier was far too disciplined an individual to ever relinquish any substantial control of power.

Bill Bennett could never stand completely above the fray. In spite of his aloofness during these years—and possibly because of it—he was never able to acquire the kind of public acclaim or recognition that other successful politicians base careers upon. The NDP, recognizing the premier's image problem, developed a political strategy of attacking Bennett personally, capitalizing on his lack of popularity. The result was perhaps the most vindictive manifestation of the politics of personality yet witnessed in British Columbia. A confidential NDP election strategy paper distributed late in 1985 outlined the reasons for such an approach:

> You will note throughout this paper that we refer to the Bennett government as opposed to the Socreds or Social Credit government. Indications are that a great many Socreds agree that the Bennett government has failed, in particular younger people who may have voted Socred in the past.
>
> If we focus our attack on Socreds, we make it more difficult for these former Socred voters to vote New Democrat. We want to rally them to the fact that the Bennett government has failed and that many other former Socred voters share this view and will be voting New Democratic in the next provincial election.
>
> This view that the Bennett government has failed is so strong in all corners of the province and with all voter groups, that we should make part of the next campaign a referendum on the Bennett government. Do they pass or fail? Our polling indicates this is the weakest point in the government's armour.

The opposition party thus launched into a brutal attack on Bill Bennett. With newspaper and television ads they decried "the Bennett record of lost jobs, lost hope." They said "Bennett's school cuts are hurting our children and our province," and "the Bennett government is killing our forests, our communities, and thousands of jobs," and "the Bennett government has failed women in B.C." Bob Skelly, following not leading his party, later revealed that he opposed this strategy, but felt he had to go along with it because the majority of the NDP provincial executive supported it.

Bennett was well aware of the NDP's approach. His office had been leaked a copy of their strategy paper. Following two by-election defeats in 1984, one in the safe Socred riding of Okanagan North, the premier started talking about renewal. At party meetings and conventions he urged new membership drives throughout the province. Principal Secretary Bud Smith spearheaded a move to attract young people to the Social Credit Party—some referred to this as the "yuppie movement." In the spring of 1986 Smith returned to his home in Kamloops, where he announced that he would seek a Socred nomination for the next provincial election.

Bennett was coy about the timing of an election. Party president Hope Wotherspoon several times requested permission to proceed with nominations, but was turned down by the premier, who was not ready to start that process. He had interviewed all of his cabinet ministers and asked them about their intentions to seek reelection, and in February of 1986 he staged a cabinet shuffle that retired some loyal veterans and hurt some tender feelings. Cabinet ministers Don Phillips and Jim Chabot were put out to pasture. Bill Bennett vividly remembered the defeat of his father's government in 1972 and how W. A. C.'s cabinet had grown old together. He desperately wished to avoid the mistakes of the past and aggressively pushed forward on his renewal theme.

Bennett's efforts were stymied and overshadowed by a string of political scandals that befell his administration. Late in 1985 Industry Minister Bob McClelland had been implicated in a Victoria prostitution trial, where it was revealed that he had used an escort agency. In January of 1986 it had been discovered that Forests Minister Tom Waterland held a $20,000 investment in a pulp company partnership. Although this investment had been disclosed for some time on his MLA's disclosure statement, it would now result in Waterland's resignation from cabinet. Soon it was revealed that Energy Minister Stephen Rogers held a $100,000 investment in the same pulp company partnership, which was not properly identified under the Financial Disclosure Act. Rogers resigned from cabinet, went to trial and received an absolute discharge. Waterland was subsequently reappointed to cabinet, but Rogers would never again serve as a Bennett minister. It was also discovered that Finance Minister Hugh Curtis had bought and sold shares in B.C. Rail, a crown corporation. At the end of January Health Minister Jim Nielsen was beaten up by his mistress's former husband. His black eye was yet another public shiner for Bennett's government. And this was followed by the revelation in March that Housing Minister Jack Kempf was living in a subsidized housing project in which he had installed a hot tub.

Although none of these scandals or embarrassments ever touched the premier directly, they did create an uneasy political

mood in the provincial capital. There was a sense that the sloppi-
ness in the personal lives of cabinet ministers and the lack of crisp-
ness in their actions was evidence that the Bennett government
was growing tired. The premier never panicked in the face of these
events; experience told him to be patient. He felt genuine
empathy for some of his colleagues and absolute disdain for the
ignorance of others. And he increased both the frequency and
urgency of his calls for Social Credit renewal.

In the fall of 1985 Kim Campbell, a young Vancouver lawyer,
former chairman of the Vancouver school board and unsuccessful
Social Credit candidate, had joined the premier's office as executive director. It seemed an unfocussed time for the government
and its leader. Campbell said:

> There wasn't a process in place to do a lot of new and innovative
> things. A couple of times Norman Spector commented to me that
> things were atypical. I didn't get the feeling that the premier had a
> large number of things that he wanted to accomplish. I didn't get
> the sense of a major policy agenda. He was just finishing projects. I
> had a sense that he was finishing off a lot of things that were impor-
> tant to him.

One of those projects was Expo 86, which opened in spectacular
fashion on 2 May at B.C. Place stadium. The opening ceremonies
were attended by the Prince and Princess of Wales, Prime Minister
Mulroney and a host of others. Premier Bennett gave a stirring
speech. And Expo chairman Jimmy Pattison received the loudest
ovation. The much-heralded world's fair got off to a dazzling start.

Another important project was the Coquihalla highway. As a
young man in Kelowna Bill Bennett had joined with chamber of
commerce members and others to promote the Coquihalla as an
important route between the coast and the province's hinterland.
But most people doubted that it would ever be built. Early on in
his premiership, Bennett committed the government to building
the highway, but engineering delays and the restraint program mil-
itated against the project. Frustrated by this lack of progress and
with a keen eye on his own future, in 1984 Bennett ordered an acceleration of the highway's construction so that it would be open in
time for Expo 86. The premier also announced that users of the
new highway would pay a toll—a practice not seen in British

Columbia since W. A. C. Bennett had abolished highway tolls more than twenty years earlier.

Bennett saw the new highway as a confidence-builder for a province that had been severely battered by the uncontrollable forces of the recession. Furthermore, in the year of Vancouver's Expo celebrations, it was extremely important for the government to spend political capital outside of the Greater Vancouver area. In addition, the highway was an event of symbolic importance for Bill Bennett: it was both a continuation of his father's vision of opening up the province's interior and an acceptance of the fact that highways and politics remain closely intertwined in British Columbia.

The premier was adamant that the forecasted $250-million first phase of the Coquihalla highway open on time. And on 16 May 1986, as his open yellow convertible sped along the virgin blacktop on the inaugural drive, Bill Bennett was a happy man. The usually unsmiling premier smiled all day long, through the official opening, the speeches, the receptions. Bennett later remarked: "It was completed and no one could stop it. I've done something that people dreamed about, but they never believed it would happen. It's done. And it's going to have long-lasting economic benefits." On that day the premier was heard to say, "I can now die happily."

Many believed that the opening of the Coquihalla highway, coming two weeks after the highly successful launching of Expo 86, was a kickoff to the long-awaited provincial election. And many of Bennett's cabinet colleagues would remember the premier, in the days following the inauguration of the Coquihalla, repeating his claim that he could "now die happily."

CHAPTER 3

Who Fired Bill Bennett?

On 22 May 1986, while many observers were awaiting an election call, Bill Bennett surprised virtually everyone in British Columbia by announcing his retirement from politics. That his announcement was so completely unexpected reveals much about our attitudes towards political leaders: we do not expect them to leave office voluntarily, especially when times are good. For several months the premier had been preaching the theme of renewal, yet no one suspected that by renewal he had meant as well a change of party leader.

But for Bennett it was far from a snap decision. Clearly he had paid a great deal of attention to the timing of his retirement and to the question of succession. In fact for some time he and his wife, Audrey, had been secretly experimenting with retirement. The previous fall they had rented a condominium in Palm Desert, and for several months the well-tanned premier had commuted from California, where his wife had joined the tennis leagues.

The first of his colleagues to hear the news was Norman Spector and, soon after, Jerry Lampert, who had only recently replaced Bud Smith as Bennett's principal secretary. Spector joined that meeting and the three discussed how Bennett should announce his decision the following day. Said Lampert:

Bennett had thought that out very much to his own liking. We had to prepare for that week's cabinet meeting. He had obviously talked this over with Norman, because he turned to me and said: "Now, here's what we want you to do, Jerry. *You* are going to go in and tell cabinet."

And I said: "What?"

He said: "You're going to tell cabinet, because I'm going to Vancouver to meet Hope Wotherspoon as party president so we can begin the process of putting together a leadership convention."

I said: "Premier, *you've* got to tell the cabinet."

And he turned to Norman and Norman said to me: "You've got to do it."

And I didn't pursue it any further than that, but it did not sit right with me.

Early the next morning the premier also called Socred fund raiser Mike Burns to notify him and ask him to set up a lunch with the Top 20. Burns remembered:

We'd been speculating that he was going to go to the polls. And we knew there was something funny going on. Breakfast meetings? Bill Bennett does not have breakfast with anyone. You know how he had breakfast? It's coffee outside the door. He won't even see the bellboy. But he had scheduled the breakfast, and then this call came about seven. He said: "Hello, this is the premier. I'm announcing my retirement today at ten o'clock."

I said: "Oh shit!"

He said: "What kind of a response is that? You should be happy for me."

Bennett met with Wotherspoon at 7:30 that morning. The party president was hoping to receive the signal to proceed with preparations for an election campaign. Instead, Bennett asked her to organize a leadership convention before the summer was over. "I was shocked," Wotherspoon said. "I thought for a minute and I said, 'Well, you're certainly not giving us very much time. And what do you want to step down for?' "

Bennett was adamant that the party—without interference from the Socred cabinet or caucus—should run the leadership conven-

tion. This was one of the reasons why he had been so secretive before his announcement. For his own part, he did not presume to be
able to choose a successor. He may have had his favourites, but he
knew very well that the independent, populist nature of his party
would make it impossible for him to anoint the next Social Credit
leader. That would be a grassroots decision. The premier had,
however, given a lot of thought to the venue for the convention
and had chosen the posh resort village of Whistler, ninety minutes
north of Vancouver. The upbeat setting of Whistler would provide
few distractions to the sharp focus of the leadership event. Whistler was an appropriate venue, for in so many respects the resort
was a creation of the Socred government and a playground for the
political and business elite of the province—and for British Columbians there can be no more serious adult game than politics. (B.C.
Hydro, which had booked the Whistler convention centre for an
economic conference at the end of July, suspiciously changed its
dates—evidence to many of foreknowledge on the part of select
Socred insiders.)

Even the date of Bennett's retirement announcement was based
upon consideration for his successor: "I worked back from when I
thought we could have a convention and leave the new leader the
option of going to an election before Expo ended or just after as a
first choice. The convention would have to be at the end of July."

At his hastily called press conference, the premier's message was
clear and simple: "The time to have change within political parties
is when things are good. And things are good. . . . There must be
political renewal. There must be change within parties. . . . My father stayed too long. . . . I can leave confident that there is a positive mood in British Columbia. And the party has never been in
better shape." Bewildered reporters mustered a few questions,
and each time the premier answered with a reiteration of his call for
renewal. Asked if he might consider entering federal politics, he
said: "I am retiring from public life."

In Victoria the cabinet met as usual. At ten o'clock, just as the
Vancouver news conference was getting under way, Jerry Lampert
approached the cabinet table—an unusual move, for officials
normally sat on the outer ring of the cabinet table—and read a brief
statement from the premier. For a moment there was a deathly
hush as the incredulous cabinet absorbed the news. Health Min-

ister Jim Nielsen remembered: "We had no idea. No one could believe it. Grace started to cry. Everyone was very emotional."

The anxious cabinet, at Grace McCarthy's suggestion, flew to Vancouver to be with the premier. "And that's where the real emotion happened," said Industry Minister Bob McClelland. "We spent a couple of hours telling Bill what we thought of him, and reminiscing about ten years. And that was a very emotional meeting."

Finance Minister Hugh Curtis watched the premier's announcement on television that night at home:

> I broke down, which is very rare. I just let it all pour out. I suppose it was the suddenness of it. I felt very emotionally tied to the man. I don't know that he understands that. But you can't work with a guy and trust him and be trusted for more than ten years. Otherwise you'd just drift away. You'd go.

Of the gathering that day, Bennett said:

> I think my ministers had more difficulty with that meeting than I did. My decision was in my mind so long, the steps that I'd taken to make the decision, all of the factors combined. There was no shock for me. I was with people who I would still be seeing for a few months. So, really, the only emotion I was feeling was watching them and how they reacted. But I appreciated the fact that they cared—if they all cared.
>
> A lot of things would go through their minds. Why is he leaving? Is he ill? And so on. I tried to explain all the reasons for going, but obviously imaginations were running wild and there was an emotional shock as well. And I think everybody wanted to hear it from me first-hand.

As to why he had not told them himself in the first place, Bennett said that his decision was a personal one and was not government policy. Because his resignation was as party leader, it was to the party that he made his announcement first, and then to the public. It was Lampert's role as principal secretary to announce the decision to cabinet and Norman Spector's as deputy minister to explain it to the professional bureaucrats. But Lampert added:

In my view, he did not want to become emotional in front of his colleagues. If he had gone in there, he would have had trouble going through it without breaking down. I honestly believe that. "Mr. Tough Guy," in those circumstances, would be a marshmallow. He didn't want to publicly show himself in that fashion. He's never been one to get himself caught in those kinds of situations. It's like the veneer—he doesn't want it to be removed.

The premier had lunch that day, as arranged, with select members of the Top 20. Mike Burns said: "These were guys he was comfortable with. These were guys who had supported the party. He'd made a political decision, and these were political friends. He came into the room to a standing ovation. There were short, spontaneous speeches around the table. It was the culmination of his relationship with these guys." Bennett later explained his motives for this private event:

They had done a lot for the party, and I had done nothing for them. I owed them an explanation directly. I thought it would be a good chance to put the word out through them to the gossipy Vancouver business community—which has a rumour a minute. I wanted to make sure that our people, who covered every aspect of downtown Vancouver, and who would eventually talk to the media, had my story.

In the days that followed Bennett's announcement there were rumours that ulterior motives may have played a part in his resignation. Perhaps he was sick, perhaps dying of cancer, or an alcoholic. Maybe a secret public opinion poll had showed he could not win re-election? Perhaps he had somehow been forced from office. These suggestions and many others circulated for months afterward. One prominent cabinet minister later responded to such rumours by repeating the question: "Who fired Bill Bennett?" Black humour also emerged. There was a story about Jimmy Pattison, who had developed a reputation for wielding the heavy hatchet in the executive suite at Expo 86. "Now Jimmy's gone too far," some said. "He's gone and axed the premier."

Clearly the premier's retirement mystified most observers. Many had believed Bennett would toy with history and attempt to stay on as premier for longer than his father. Most of his cabinet colleagues and nonelected officials would never come to terms

with the real reason for the premier's departure, demonstrating
how little they really understood their boss. Patrick Kinsella, for
one, had firmly believed that Bennett was going to lead the
Socreds into another election.

Every evidence pointed to that, including the fact that he had called
in his caucus one by one and said: "Are you running? If you're not, I
want to know." He implied that he was going to be there. I think all
of his colleagues thought he was going to be there. And yet, the day
he did it, he did it in typical Bill Bennett style. Bang, bang, and it
was all over. "Thank you very much. It's been great."

But I think I know the man well enough to know that on his return from the opening of the Coquihalla, he took his tie off. The job
was over. I think that's where it happened.

Jerry Lampert disagreed that the premier's decision was a spontaneous one.

Bennett was right when he said he was frustrated in trying to kick
ass to get the party mobilized to go into an election campaign. He
had tried through a membership appeal. And he had launched into
his "yuppie tour" when he sent Bud and others to go around the
province to promote the party. The yuppie tour was not really getting off the ground. And I believe that he came to the conclusion
that he couldn't renew the party. And the only thing that could
renew the party was the leadership process.

And I think it bothered him that he wasn't able to convince
people that he did in '83 what he had to do, that it made sense in the
long-term economic stability of the province. He just wasn't able to
change his image, or convince people that he did what was right, or
get people to trust him. As well, the public view of the government
was not good because of some of these scandals that were occurring.
Bennett was frustrated by that because I think he knew that he
couldn't fix that easily. He could not just fire all these guys, because
he didn't have much on the backbench to turn to.

All these things made him think for some time that maybe the
right way to renew in every sense of the word was for him to move
along.

Bud Smith was among those few who were not completely
caught off-guard by the premier's resignation. He believed that

Bennett had set everything up to give himself "absolutely maxi-
mum options to go to the people with a June election or to get
out." The premier, he said, had concluded that renewal could best
be achieved by having it start at the top.

> And that's why I say he's a very self-contained guy. That's a very,
> very difficult thing to do, to separate yourself and your ego and your
> personal achievements and your goals and your sense of self-
> importance from your understanding of what the party's need is and
> from the goals you are trying to achieve.

And Norman Spector has said: "My sense from him later was that
fundamental to his decision to retire was the question of institutionalizing the party. He had the feeling that the party was
mature enough to survive his exit."

The temptation for Bennett to seek one more electoral triumph,
a vindication of his restraint policies and a celebration of Expo 86
and other megaprojects, must have been close to overpowering.
But he did not succumb. He had once said that politics would not
be a lifetime career, and he stuck to his plan. He had made the decision to leave, and he was not about to back down on a commitment made to himself:

> The decision was made in '84, subject to certain things happening.
> That is, it was almost a prayer: "Oh God, if we can get through all of
> this and try to get the economy going and if we can contain govern-
> ment costs and show that we've stabilized the deficit, and if we get
> Expo working, and if we can do all of these things . . . If all that's
> right and at the time if I can get the party cranked up and if it's
> really working—if all these things happen, then I'm going." So
> that's when I would have made that commitment to myself.
>
> I had a dozen things that had to happen. It was a conditional deci-
> sion in my own mind. But I had made that sort of decision when I
> first entered politics—that it'd be two terms. And I sort of had that
> decision in mind when I went into '83. But I couldn't leave then.

Bill Bennett likely did not consider it a major failing to have
been unable to groom a successor to the mantle of leadership of the
Social Credit Party. Even if he had wanted to, his management
style would have provided an insurmountable obstacle. He
seemed to lead by a dictum of Havelock Ellis: "To be a leader of

men, one must turn one's back on men." Bennett spent most of his time keeping people from getting too close to him. He had no yen for intimacy.

As premier, his isolated, almost monkish lifestyle made him vulnerable to rumour and innuendo. Victoria gossip would have many believe that Bennett was a strange, quiet, conniving leader. The truth is that he was an extremely disciplined, hard-working, lonely premier. In a rare revelation, he outlined his own well-considered views on the art of leadership:

> You can't be having a cup of coffee, or playing cards, or socializing evening after evening with colleagues and still maintain that leadership role. You wouldn't do it in the private sector. You couldn't do it effectively. In government, leadership is a lonely role inasmuch as my view of it is that you have to pick a cabinet team, and for them to work well you have to be their leader. You have to be there when they need you—that's when you need to be their friend. Not their social friend. Their friend when they need you, understanding difficulties, personal or government. You have to ensure that they all have equal access, that there aren't favourites.
>
> I preferred to deal with them personally, directly. But that did not involve having lunch and dinner. I spent my time working. I was elected to be premier to work. And I made it a working premiership, not a social premiership.
>
> It was the only way I could do the job. I am not cut out for the cocktail party circuit or a lot of receptions. I would do them as part of my work. But I liked the work. In the evenings, I would take my work home if I wasn't scheduled to speak or to travel or be at a dinner. I would go home and take all of my reading, because I wanted to know as much as I could. And I wouldn't read it that night. If I had a night off, I would go to bed as early as I could and wake up at four-thirty or five o'clock in the morning, and that's when I'd do my reading.
>
> I just didn't have time for the normal, social relationships. And when I did take time it was to play tennis at 6:30 in the morning. But the responsibilities were too great. Maybe it was me. Maybe some other premier could have done the job in an eight-hour day. I couldn't.

It was Bennett's reserved leadership style and hard-working approach to the job of premier that helped create his difficult public image. A very shy man, he could not bring himself to be the populist that others demanded. He was often unavailable for comment and was typically seen running from the television cameras with a nervous, uncomfortable smile. He was considered extremely tough as a manager—in fact his critics said he was cruel and mean-spirited—but this image seems to have been a defensive shell that he purposefully hid behind. Those who worked closely with Bennett knew him as a perceptive, charming, modest man capable of inspiring strong loyalty. Even after the modernization of the Social Credit Party and the importation of some of the country's best political advisers and image makers like Patrick Kinsella, the public's perception of the premier changed little. Certainly during the restraint controversy his image hardened—but that may be attributed to a public relations ploy.

According to Grace McCarthy, during the troubled time of restraint a cadre of people close to the premier shielded him from reality and encouraged the myth that restraint had to be reinforced and that Bennett had to become stronger and even more determined in his objectives.

> And when they did that, it allowed the public to get a whole different perception of Bill Bennett—which might have been the truth and might not have been. But what resulted was an unfortunate reaction from the public. And I think Bill Bennett left office with the public saying that they probably wouldn't reinstate him. And that was unfortunate because he had given so much to the public.
>
> I think it was unfortunate in the latter years that that cadre of people who surrounded him wanted to put him into the mould of Ontario politics, the worst parts of Ontario politics which we did not like—and which, by the way, defeated the Conservative government in Ontario at just about the same time. We seemed to adopt all the worst features of the Ontario administration.

In a populist province like British Columbia, the controversial art of professional image making will always be looked upon with suspicion and fear. Bennett was definitely the author of his own style, stubbornly resisting those who tried to tamper with or improve it. Nevertheless, Kinsella later took credit for creating the premier's "tough guy" image, claiming that it was necessary to win the 1983 election, forming the foundation of the government's restraint program. According to Kinsella, Bennett was seen as a strong leader and an inflexible businessman—"not a guy you would take to a Canucks game." And the image included bad relationships with the press and, to some extent, bad relationships with his party, "because there was always someone like a Vander Zalm or someone who wanted to be God or king."

> This guy was not your typical politician. Never was. There are so many instances where he did the unpolitical thing. He is not what you and I would call a politician in the sense of the baby-kissing and the hand-shaking and the friendly smile and the Bill Vander Zalm– Brian Mulroney stuff. That never appealed to Bill Bennett. He knew he had a job to do.

So for Kinsella it was primarily a problem of marketing, and no doubt from a political viewpoint Bill Bennett did pose a monumental marketing challenge. But his tough guy image was largely of his own making—it did not require professional fabrication. Deputy Minister Norman Spector, a keen student of Bennett's leadership style, believed that the premier had to project a "certain coldness and toughness to be able to withstand the pressure that pulls on a person who is willing to think in the long term rather than in the short term and think 'Let's give them the sugar now.' "

Bennett saw as one of his greatest strengths this ability to think in the long term—to quickly absorb and assess a lot of information and from it quickly develop an overview of government direction. And having decided on the correct course, determination to follow it through was another strength, though Bennett was often criticized for this "stubbornness."

Yet while being able to think of the "big picture" was his greatest strength, Bennett saw as his greatest weakness an inability to communicate the big picture:

> The ability to take the big picture, which I thought I understood so well, and make it understandable to the average person quickly, so we could bring the public along in supporting us—I wasn't able to do that. I did not do it well. And I should have. And, yet, in time the public did come along and support what we were doing. But it was one of my weaknesses. Along with the work plan, I never put as much attention into the public information plan. I felt a sense of

urgency that couldn't wait for that. That's a weakness of mine as a leader.

In Bennett's view, the big picture was a crucial political consideration. He cared deeply about his province, its development and an economic transformation he did not wish to forestall. And his ability to lead his party and manage the provincial government was inevitably affected by the big picture. In Norman Spector's view, there are both parallels and differences in the private sector and the public sector between the roles of CEO and premier.

> Bennett did provide a sense of vision as to what his goals were, and he communicated them well to his office and to his ministers. He used cabinet as an educative tool for his ministers, to set out where he wanted to go, why we should be moving in one direction and not another, why certain issues should be given priority and not others. And there was no doubt whose overall vision of British Columbia, its place in Canada, its place in the world, was providing impetus and stimulus to the work. I think he set the agenda fairly well within the government.
>
> In terms of the differences between the public and private sector, I don't think there's any doubt that Mr. Bennett knew there was a strong difference. I think he knew that in the public sector he had a number of competing pressures: social goals, the media, the political situation. Things were not quite as direct.

W. A. C. Bennett had always been fond of saying that government was a business and should be run on sound business principles. Bill Bennett did not necessarily agree with his father's strict definition. He believed that a modern government needed to provide strong leadership in both social and economic matters while serving as a responsible employer of public servants. As a manager, he tended to rely on principles more common in the private sector than in government. His own private sector background was as an entrepreneur and risk taker, not as a corporate figurehead, and when it came to government he remained very much an entrepreneur and risk taker. He knew that the criteria for success, in the private sector as well as government, was simple—it was the bottom line. Said Bennett:

There isn't an unlimited pool of capital to finance all of the programs you'd like to bring in. So here's where you bring in business techniques. When you introduce new programs, your economists try to forecast the future growth of the economy and you try to translate that into the likely growth in revenues. And then you try to forecast the growth in costs or expansion of a program, to see if it's affordable. We brought in programs that were forecast to be affordable in the heady days of the late seventies that we cancelled in the eighties when the recession hit. The dental care program is an example. Under normal planning these programs would have been sustainable.

The whole thing comes down to not just being good administrators or good managers—politicians never are—but what you are going to do as managers and policy developers about where the province is going to go. And you have to have your overall plan. And you have to be able to adjust your goals within stream. You have to look at the seventies on one side, when there was a climate of everything can happen, we can have anything we want, we don't have to pay for it, unlimited demands for wages, unlimited awarding of compensation contracts, double digit, 20 per cent, 30 per cent. Government, going from that climate, has to lead the change of social attitudes, public understanding. You can't keep selling over-expectation.

People in my party used to ask me: "Can't you give us some good news?" A leadership role is one where you have to tell the people the facts, you have to sometimes help lower expectations, given a sense of reality. You have to bring that reality to government which is already in the private sector. And that's difficult. I was under pressure from a lot of my own colleagues to give good news: "Stop using the word *restraint*. Stop making tough speeches."

And the worst thing I would see in the period we're coming into now is if they raise the level to over-expectation again. People are in a good, realistic mood in this province. And that can be thrown away very easily. It's hard to win. People don't need to be oversold. They don't need the glitter. The mood I think they're in is: "If we work hard, can we grow? Can we have some opportunity for increases in values? Will my home be safe? We know that the crazy days of inflation did not provide real prosperity. Give us some confidence."

They understand all that. Don't sell them back to those expectations, because they can't be met. I think the people of B.C. are probably more realistic than anywhere else in Canada.

Bennett found the job of lowering public expectations "painful." Although his administration had a reputation for being too tough on the poor and disadvantaged, each year it spent an increasing percentage of the provincial budget on social services, health and education. Bennett left behind a more comprehensive health care system, a larger community college network and fewer pupils for every teacher in B.C. classrooms than when he assumed office in 1975. Nevertheless, high unemployment and food-bank lineups were all-too-visible signs of the province's restructuring economy during his troubled years.

Still, Bennett was a pioneer in the advocacy and pursuit of reducing government. Even if it was only the methods for achieving his goals that one argued with, his bias for action cannot be denied. Only a Margaret Thatcher or a Ronald Reagan could claim to have attacked the size, cost and scope of government as vigorously. Canadian leaders distanced themselves from this approach, fearing the political cost of "doing a Bennett." Some of them would later pay dearly for failing to come to terms with fundamental economic change.

As contentious as the restraint program was the government's encouragement of megaprojects that resulted in the needed infrastructure for further industrial development. Critics argued that such an economic strategy was shortsighted, failed to address the social needs of British Columbians, and swallowed up vast public funds that could be better spent elsewhere.

Grace McCarthy saw Bennett's premiership as clearly divided into two sections. The first was when he wanted to make his mark and the economy was such that he was able to do so. Those, she said, were the days of the adventurous megaprojects, days of making decisions for the future.

And then there was the second part of his administration when he was dogged by a world recession which really made him defensive against something that was not of his own doing. Then he became a very proud leader against governments that were spending taxpayers' dollars in times when they shouldn't have been. And he was encouraged by the Canadian media because they perceived him to be brave in the face of protests from the public.

Leaving aside all the controversies, all the policies, all the dominant themes in British Columbia's politics and business life during his years, perhaps Bill Bennett's most underrated megaproject was the Social Credit Party itself. Social Credit, because of its history or its name or its regional base, had never been completely accepted, and with the NDP success in 1972 the party was widely assumed to be finished as a viable political force. The younger Bennett was determined to leave behind a stronger and more accepted party, a party which would outlive any single leader, indeed which would outlive the Bennetts. He made the institutionalization of his party his greatest goal. That he successfully achieved that goal cannot be denied. Bennett said:

> Because of what we've done and because of Expo, in B.C. today people are proud to be Socreds. For the first time, business people individually have chosen to be involved. And they've been criticized for it because they're not supposed to be able to stand up and say they're Socreds, or there must be something wrong. There isn't anything wrong. There's been a change. Social Credit has come of age. It's matured. It's understood.

The argument about Social Credit as a party versus Social Credit as a coalition also has strong implications for the kind of leadership appropriate to it. In Bennett's view:

> Coalitions break up. I watched the coalition between the Liberals and the Conservatives break up. As soon as it served their partisan interests to break up, they did. So they couldn't work to the full good of the province with complete trust in each other in government. Coalitions can never provide good government, because their ultimate aim is to defeat each other. I knew that. I had watched my father, who realized it when he was a member and tried to turn the coalition into a party.
>
> Social Credit isn't a coalition. You have to buy a membership and you have to make a commitment. You are a British Columbia Social Credit Party member. It really is a party.
>
> A coalition implies a multiplicity of leadership. A party can only have one leader. You may not like your leader—and then you change him. But you can only have one. Coalitions of convenience always break up because they have a number of leaders each with their own game plan, each with their own set of priorities. And it's always bargaining, bargaining, bargaining.
>
> The political process itself is bargaining—but not from a precon-

ceived set of positions from which trade-offs are achieved. Personal
trade-offs, but never power blocs. Coalitions have never been effective over a long period of time. And I've always viewed Social Credit
as a political vehicle that can change with the times without sacrific-
ing its basic philosophy, without requiring great political shifts and
heaves. It can be a political vehicle that can make changes within
itself.

Bill Bennett's decision to step down tested this assumption
about Social Credit's maturity. It also gave him an opportunity to
seriously assess his own development as a leader, politician and
person:

I've had an extensive education, both practical and academic, after
all the research and reading and experience. But over and above
that, I had some growing to do as a person as I sorted out where I
was going. And that happened at the same time as I grew politically.
I learned to handle people and events and situations better. And by
the end, the reason you don't get rattled by the press any more is
you've seen it all and you know it never lasts. All you can do is, you
can keep it a three-day story, or a week story or, if you really fumble
it, you can turn it into a three-week story. I probably was better
equipped when I left to do a really good job as premier than in any
of the other years. I was better prepared in everything—other than
youth and vigour—than I ever was. Except I'd been around for thirteen years. It was time for a change.

On 17 June 1986 Bennett made his final major address in the
legislature that had so terribly intimidated him as a freshman MLA.
He had now mastered the imposing legislature, becoming the most
effective debater in the House. In fact, he could alter the mood of
the place and the tenor of the debate simply by entering the legislative chamber. Looking younger and more at ease than ever before, he defended the spending estimates for the premier's office—funds that would be spent by a yet unknown successor—in a
memorable, even graceful speech. And he concluded with a plea
for tough criticism, not kindness, upon his departure:

I am pleased to have served with all of you. I appreciate your contribution, and especially the criticism of the opposition. I don't want to

end on too nice a note. I will miss certain aspects of this legislature, and so to start you off, I would like to remember some of the names that you might call me, just so I won't feel I'm leaving un-remembered. You might call me Mini-Wac. You might call me a dictator, a wimp, Three-dollar Bill. You might call me a leader that can't control his cabinet, or you might call me someone who never listens to his ministers or his backbench. You could call us a jackboot government. Please, one more time before I go, I would like to hear those words.

At the end of July he attended the Socred leadership convention at Whistler. Still premier, Bennett kept a low profile, aside from an emotional farewell to him as party leader on the opening evening. During those few dramatic days at Whistler, many Social Credit delegates suggested to Bennett that he was making a mistake by retiring. His consistent response was: "Just wait. Six months down the road you'll understand. You will believe I did the right thing." This cryptic answer reflected his belief that the new leader would call an election within six months of the leadership convention and thereby demonstrate the benefits of renewal.

After submitting his resignation to the lieutenant governor on 6 August, Bennett put in a brief appearance at a small press reception in the parliament buildings. When the ex-premier strode into the lounge, one reporter cracked, "Oh, it's nice to see an ordinary citizen for a change."

"No, no," said Bennett, "I'm still the MLA for Okanagan South."

Norman Spector, retiring as deputy minister to the premier, playfully asked, "Okanagan South? Where's that?"

"Just follow the pavement," smiled Bennett.

Bill Bennett played to win, and he left public life a winner.

CHAPTER 4

Father, Son and Holy Ghost

What Tolstoy said about families, that "all happy families resemble each other while each unhappy family is unhappy in its own way," turns out to be true for political parties as well. Successful parties, especially those firmly entrenched in government, typically demonstrate a discipline of power that suggests the unity and strength of a happy family. On the other hand, political parties stuck for too long in the despair of opposition show signs of the quarreling, bickering and infighting evident in unhappy and fragmented families.

Bill Bennett's Social Credit family in British Columbia did not resemble other "happy families," nor did it appear unhappy in its uniqueness. However, when Bennett announced his retirement with a call for renewal, he opened floodgates of ambition and disaffection within his party, his family. His unquestioned leadership, it seemed, had camouflaged a deep but silent restlessness. The race to succeed him as Social Credit leader—and premier—would display clashes of egos among family members and would reveal envy, bitterness and fear. It would also promote considerable interest and enthusiasm, attracting many new members to the party and quickening the pulses of long-time Socreds.

In the spring of 1986 the party had been gearing up for an expected election campaign and was ill-prepared for only the second leadership convention in its history. Leadership conventions at which party members or delegates choose a new leader are recent phenomena in Canadian political life. Fifty years ago leaders were chosen by the legislative caucus of their party, in the same way as the British Conservative Party continues to do. Since then, leadership conventions have become institutionalized in Canada as an essential part of our politics, not only because they are seen as a democratic way to choose a leader but also because they strengthen a party's organization and public perception if properly organized. Because most political parties experience the joys and the trauma of leadership succession only once or twice in a generation, each leadership convention is an invaluable learning exercise.

With only nine weeks to organize a convention, the Socred party hastily shifted into high gear. The party bylaws contained only two paragraphs about leadership conventions, and those said very little. Party president Hope Wotherspoon recalled: "The convention committee literally wrote rules every day. And then we had to make sure they were legal. Then the board had to meet to ratify every rule. Our committee met for sixteen, eighteen, twenty hours a day. There wasn't time to make mistakes."

(Several key party officials, instead of remaining neutral as convention organizers, were lured into partisanship for leadership hopefuls, further hampering the party's preparations. For instance, David Marley, the party's executive director, quit his post to work on Brian Smith's campaign. And as soon as Bill Vander Zalm announced his candidacy, MLA Rita Johnston left her position on the convention central committee to work on his campaign.)

The process of choosing political leadership reveals much about a party and its attitude towards democracy. Unlike the practice of virtually all other Canadian parties, which confer automatic delegate status to a range of party elite members, executive functionaries and power blocs, the distinguishing feature of the Socred succession of leadership was that, save for elected MLAs, there was no automatic voting status for any party member. The Socred leader would be chosen by thirteen hundred delegates elected from each provincial constituency.

This system put tremendous pressure on the delegate selection process. Elections for delegates were generally hotly contested, and the tug of loyalties and debts of allegiance pulled on the consciences of party members; perhaps up to half the delegates elected to vote at Whistler were, at the outset, uncommitted or undeclared.

In the days following Bill Bennett's retirement announcement, many names were mentioned as potential candidates for leadership. Within the Social Credit Party it was speculated that several cabinet ministers might throw their hats into the ring, including Jim Nielsen, Hugh Curtis, Brian Smith and Grace McCarthy. Other Socred MLAs openly expressing interest in the job were former Tory MP John Reynolds, and Stephen Rogers, who earlier in the year had been removed from cabinet over conflict of interest charges. A former Socred MLA and now Conservative MP, Bob Wenman, signalled a possible return to British Columbia from Ottawa. Others put forward as having sufficient profile or interest in the job were: former Liberal MP, former mayor of Vancouver and now Critical Industries Commissioner Art Phillips; chairman of Canarim Investment, Peter Brown; chairman of the Bank of British Columbia, Edgar Kaiser Jr., and, basking in a strong glow of popularity, Expo 86 Chairman Jimmy Pattison.

Pattison's name led the private polls. The success of the world's fair had made the Vancouver businessman a local legend as a man who got things done. Never having been elected to anything before was not an apparent liability—it certainly did not hamper his personal popularity. For Pattison, the pressure to consider entering public life was as intense as the prospect was tempting. Despite the urgings of senior Socreds and the supportive results of the polls, Pattison twice declined to enter the race, citing severe conflict of interest with his business.

The most controversial of the possible candidates were Bill Vander Zalm and Bud Smith. Vander Zalm had left Victoria three years earlier, but with a promise to return. (During his self-proclaimed sabbatical he had lost a disastrous bid for the mayoralty of Vancouver.) Whereas most potential candidates were at first cautiously noncommittal about the possibility of entering the race, Vander Zalm was characteristically forthcoming: "I've always had a desire to take on any challenge and challenging positions, so it's obviously there. I'm involved in a number of things at this time and I can say I need to give it a lot of thought."

In the days following the premier's retirement, latent and overt suspicion focussed on his former principal secretary, Bud Smith. Smith had left the premier's office that spring to seek a nomination for the next provincial election in his home town of Kamloops. Earlier he had spearheaded a major Socred membership drive, dubbed the "yuppie tour." Within Social Credit, Smith was seen as a strong Bennett loyalist and a protégé of the premier. Now it seemed to many party insiders, especially cabinet ministers, that when Bennett had spoken of renewal, he had been referring to the 40-year-old Smith. Although Bud Smith had never held elective office, he quickly emerged as the front runner in the race. The rumours of his candidacy were fuelled by party president Hope Wotherspoon's unwitting comment to a news reporter that the renewal process could best be fulfilled by attracting the "Bud Smiths of the world" into the party.

It is impossible to prove a conspiracy of succession. Bud Smith admitted that he had not been surprised by Premier Bennett's announcement, but added that neither would he have been surprised by the dropping of an election writ. Bennett later defended the presumptuousness of Smith's candidacy by saying: "It was presumptuous for me when I ran for leader to think I could be leader." Jerry Lampert, who succeeded Smith as the premier's principal secretary, suggested that if Bennett had seriously wanted to groom Bud as a successor, he would have run one more election. Lampert added: "I can only say that Bill Bennett would have, in my view, been very, very happy if Bud had won."

Although the truth will never be known, the shape, the tone and indeed the outcome of the Social Credit leadership race was significantly affected by the belief that a small, elite group of insiders had decided the fate of the race before the starting pistol had been fired. This perception was strongest amongst members of the cabinet, most of whom were still mystified and miffed over the premier's retirement and the secrecy preceding its announcement. Said Jim Nielsen: "I didn't shovel shit in the stables for ten years to have someone else come in and ride the pony."

Nielsen, like so many other cabinet ministers who were potential contenders for the party leadership, had been discredited in a recent scandal. And like so many others, he was contacted by Bud Smith's backers and told that he would be a valued member of their team. It was even suggested that he would stay in cabinet. He retorted: "Why would I *not* remain in cabinet?" He talked to Bud Smith before he declared his candidacy and asked: "Why are you in such a hurry? Why don't you run and become an MLA first?"

Smith responded: "People have persuaded me that I could do the job." Nielsen said: "I'm not questioning your ability. But why are you in such a hurry?"

Nielsen felt strongly that Bill Bennett's successor should be an elected member of the party. Now, in the face of an apparent scheme by nonelected outsiders to win the mantle of leadership, it seemed that while no one was ruling themselves out of the contest, neither was there a mad rush to enter. He spoke with several members of cabinet and caucus and found that "nobody was challenging what appeared to be this machine."

He told Attorney General Brian Smith: "If you announce today that you're running, then I'll announce that I'm backing you." But there was no announcement that day. A frustrated Nielsen also spoke to his friend and former cabinet minister Stephen Rogers, who, after some thought, called Nielsen to say that he was not running but would back him. In this confusing quagmire of indecision, and sparked by outrage over the imminent announcement of Bud Smith's intention to seek the party leadership, Nielsen entered the race on 4 June. "Something had to be done to stop what I thought was an improper campaign."

Jim Nielsen's candidacy mustered some strong caucus support, but his hope that his colleagues might rally around him proved naive. Prior to Nielsen, only one other candidate had declared: MLA John Reynolds. Reynolds had little to lose by quickly announcing his bid for the leadership. The former Conservative MP had been lounging on the backbench and this was an opportunity for province-wide recognition. Reynolds, however, was dogged by rumours and unproven allegations of past connections to organized crime.

Two days after Nielsen, cabinet minister Bill Ritchie entered the race. The wealthy businessman from the Fraser Valley would add some colour to the race, but his candidacy would not gain widespread support. A few days later, Stephen Rogers announced his candidacy, confusing Nielsen. Rogers later admitted that the general uncertainty over who might run was one factor behind his decision. More important, he added, "I was really running to rebuild my own dignity, because I felt I had been dealt a very bad hand."

The same day, Conservative MP Bob Wenman entered the fray. Wenman had been a young Socred MLA back in the days of

W. A. C. Bennett and was now attempting to fashion a return to provincial politics. Also that day, Bud Smith put an end to all the speculation by formally announcing his candidacy. And the following day, Socred backbencher Cliff Michael and Saanich mayor Mel Couvelier joined the battle.

On 12 June, a surprise to many, Socred executive director Kim Campbell announced her intention to run. At thirty-nine, she was the youngest contender for the crown; her candidacy was not taken altogether seriously by many party members, but she would add a much needed intellectual dimension to the process of Social Credit renewal.

Kim Campbell's declaration was overshadowed by Grace McCarthy's simultaneous announcement that she would indeed seek the leadership. Her announcement significantly changed the complexion of the leadership race, for she inspired strong loyalties among many party members. It was suggested that she was running to serve as a king-maker at the leadership convention, but Grace McCarthy vehemently denied this. She was in the race to win. She said later she had wondered whether she could make the long-term commitment required of a leader. "Then I realized I didn't have any choice. I had to make that commitment," she said, referring to the apparent conspiracy of succession. "There is no question there was a plan, and the plan went awry."

McCarthy was motivated both by powerful instincts for the preservation of the party that she had helped to build and a sense of anger directed towards those who seemed to disregard the virtues of hard work, trust and experience as the only legitimate prerequisites for leadership.

Bud Smith was the focus of a great deal of criticism during the early part of the leadership campaign. However, for McCarthy, Nielsen and a host of prominent Socreds, he was merely representative of an unwelcome element in their party: the Ontario-based Big Blue Machine, which threatened the populist traditions of Social Credit in British Columbia. The most recognized, most brilliant and perhaps most distrusted member of this political elite was Patrick Kinsella. Kinsella and Smith, both former principal secretaries to Bill Bennett, shared a mutual respect, but did not see eye-to-eye on many matters of B.C. politics, and Kinsella did not back Smith in the leadership sweepstakes.

When Bud Smith announced his candidacy, Kinsella was a campaign manager in search of a candidate—"I was looking around for how in my own little way to what extent I could influence the choice of the next leader." Concluding that someone from outside the party could probably win, he talked to several potential candidates from the Vancouver business community and commissioned polling data on their public recognition factors. Kinsella particularly encouraged Art Phillips. The critical industries commissioner had a positive public image and no apparent liabilities; however, he wisely decided against an attempt at winning the leadership of a party he had never belonged to.

Kinsella found his candidate not in an outsider but in Attorney General Brian Smith, the last cabinet minister and eleventh candidate to enter the race. Brian Smith was a credible but non-charismatic contender who would be able to draw support from the Social Credit caucus as well as from the federal Tories within the provincial governing party. He was perceived as a potential compromise candidate, and Kinsella set to work running a fast-paced and well-managed campaign promoting his man in this fashion—a kind of "Bill Davis comes to B.C." campaign.

The Brian Smith who emerged on the way to Whistler—lively, smiling, well-groomed and fastidiously dressed—was in large part a creation of Pat Kinsella's. And for many Socreds this candidate would never emerge from the shadow of his controversial campaign manager, who was also out to make his own mark during the contest. Kinsella recalled warning the attorney general that he was going to be a big issue in the campaign; he wanted Smith to understand the baggage he would be carrying with him. Kinsella believed he could get his man to the last ballot at the convention but was afraid of one possible development. Kinsella shared with Brian Smith some confidential polling data of delegates to the previous year's Social Credit convention. The poll asked the delegates, of whom seven out of ten would be voting at Whistler, whom they would support for the party leadership. "And Bill Vander Zalm led everyone two-to-one," recalled Kinsella. "There was no one even close!"

As controversial as the candidates in this race were their hired helpers. The leadership race brought some of the best political organizers in the country to British Columbia. Most campaigns were

made up largely of volunteers with a few paid political professionals directing traffic and strategy. Patrick Kinsella was perhaps the
most high profile helper in evidence, but he was competing against
a field of other pros and enthusiastic amateurs. Bill Gaulton, an
experienced Tory organizer from Newfoundland, managed Bob
Wenman's campaign. The legendary John Laschinger arrived on
the west coast scene to handle Bud Smith's leadership effort.
Lasch, as he was called, was also an alumnus of the Ontario Big
Blue Machine and had managed John Crosbie's attempt to win the
federal Conservative leadership. Whistler was his sixth leadership
campaign, and this wealth of experience inspired both awe and
fear in other candidates' camps.

On the way to Whistler an interesting variety of myths and fables
concerning supposed strengths, weaknesses and alliances were
nurtured among the candidates, their supporters and the media: an
agreement between Bud Smith and Brian Smith to support each
other come hell or high water (the Smith Bros. Great Cough Drop
Conspiracy); a pact between McCarthy and Vander Zalm (the
McZalm theory); McCarthy's support was soft (the Flora syndrome
comes to B.C.); the governing party would never choose a
maverick like Vander Zalm (the Stop Vander Zalm movement);
and a coalition amongst the Caucus Five—Jim Nielsen, John
Reynolds, Stephen Rogers, Bill Ritchie and Cliff Michael—to
support whomever finished first amongst their group (the Fifth
Man theory).

These and other scenarios and subplots were played out a thousand times over on the way to Whistler. Most of them had some
grounds for justification or contained grains of truth; all of them
would be proven false in the rush of excitement at Whistler. One
certainty, however, was that four of the twelve candidates had
pulled far ahead of the pack.

The campaigns of Bud Smith and Brian Smith both stressed
moderate, modern approaches to politics and government, with
high-tech strategies and consensus styles of leadership. The chief
difference was that Brian Smith was an elected cabinet minister
and Bud Smith was an outsider, a former backroom boy. Although
he remained officially neutral, it was believed that Bennett could
support either of these candidates.

Neither Bud Smith nor Brian Smith were charismatic leaders,
nor were they overtly populist; both laboured behind the auras of

their controversial campaign managers. Indeed, the fencing and strategic manoeuvring between Patrick Kinsella and John Laschinger added an extra strategic dimension to the leadership contest. Both campaign managers looked for every possible advantage, operating under a widespread assumption that the Smith who finished ahead of the other on the first ballot would receive the support of his namesake.

The Smiths ran the two most polished and professional campaigns and together received the lion's share of support from the party establishment. Brian Smith's Vancouver Island base of delegate support seemed uncertain, but with Kinsella's organizational skills and the prospect of caucus and cabinet colleagues rallying around him, he was a force to reckon with. Bud Smith's delegate support came largely from the interior of the province, the traditional Social Credit stronghold. As a newcomer, though, he had assembled a surprisingly strong team of supporters, including former cabinet minister Peter Hyndman, former party president and widow of Hugh Harris, Meldy Harris, cabinet ministers Alex Fraser and Tom Waterland, and former cabinet minister Don Phillips.

Ahead of the Smiths was Grace McCarthy, who dubbed her campaign Operation Grassroots in a direct challenge to the slick professionalism of the Smiths' campaigns. She enjoyed strong support from the Social Credit old guard and was a front runner from the moment she entered the race: cabinet ministers Elwood Veitch, Pat McGeer, Garde Gardom, Jack Kempf and Hugh Curtis would be at her side along with MLAs Doug Mowat and Angus Ree. Although she was considered to be in first place or a close second as the leadership convention approached, her appeal to a wider constituency was blocked by the rumour that she and Bill Vander Zalm were effectively running mates. This was the "McZalm theory."

Most everyone had doubted that Vander Zalm would declare his candidacy. A short campaign favoured those contestants who got off to a quick start, and over a week after the first candidate had declared, Vander Zalm was still silent. Furthermore, he was deeply involved in the financing and construction of his multi-million-dollar tourist attraction in Richmond—Fantasy Gardens—and he had confided to many that it was unlikely he would be able to relinquish his responsibilities. He also doubted that he could garner sufficient support. After his "gutless" comment, he was seen to be a renegade and had had very little contact with Victoria politics for three years. His vacillating now forced many potential supporters to look elsewhere for a leader.

Socred MLA Rita Johnston, for example, had always believed that one day Vander Zalm would seek the premiership, "but I think it was about four years sooner than what he probably thought would suit his schedule." Several times she encouraged Vander Zalm to run, but eventually gave up and started to serve on the convention election committee.

Long-time Socred Charlie Giordano called Vander Zalm two days after Bill Bennett's retirement announcement and encouraged him to run. Vander Zalm was undecided. Giordano had many lengthy and repetitive discussions with him at Fantasy Gardens, reviewing the pros and cons of contesting the leadership and assessing his chances of victory. "Meantime he would be answering calls and on his desk there would be stacks and stacks of pink and yellow message slips." Invariably these were calls urging Vander Zalm to run. He would coyly ask Giordano: "Well, why do you think I should run?" Giordano would fire back: "I think the mess on your desk should tell you that. All these people want you to run."

Vander Zalm's business adviser and owner of the White Spot restaurant chain, Peter Toigo, wanted Vander Zalm to go for the leadership but told him: "It's absolutely wrong for where you are in your business career at this time to separate yourself from this business. Absolutely, you should not run." Vander Zalm agreed with this advice, but confessed that he seriously wanted to contest the party leadership.

Vander Zalm took his time, luxuriating in the attention brought on by his indecision. When it came down to the crunch, on 19 June, Vander Zalm asked Giordano to draft a news release stating that he would not enter the leadership race because of potential conflicts with his business. That evening he told Peter Toigo of his decision that it was over. "And I felt it *was* over," recalled Toigo.

Giordano was writing the last paragraph when Vander Zalm phoned him. "Throw it away," Vander Zalm told him. "We're going to go for it. Do another release for ten o'clock tomorrow morning." He had decided to ignore both his own judgement and the best advice he had received and followed his instincts instead.

Two hours before the announcement, he told Toigo of his change of mind. Somewhat flabbergasted, Toigo said, "Just run. We'll sort everything out. And just run." Radio station executive John Plul visited Vander Zalm at Fantasy Gardens ten minutes before the announcement. Although a friend of Vander Zalm's, Plul had committed himself to work on Grace McCarthy's campaign. He had come to find out what Vander Zalm would be announcing, hoping that he would not enter the race. "It was the split that I was worried about," Plul later said. He feared that Bill Vander Zalm would draw support from delegates backing Grace McCarthy. Plul was surprised and disappointed by Vander Zalm's decision.

It is possible that Vander Zalm purposefully left his decision until the last possible moment to fuel speculation and interest in his candidacy, although such a strategy was extremely risky. Vander Zalm said: "I can't take credit for being that bright." But he also indicated that hesitation could not hurt his chances. "I felt all along that I wasn't as pushed as others might have been. And it didn't hurt me to leave it a while. In fact it helped, because then the campaign was: 'Come on, Vander Zalm, why don't you run?' "

Vander Zalm later said it was McCarthy who had convinced him. She was worried about Bud Smith's growing support, believing that Bennett and other powerful party members were backing him. Her view was that she and Vander Zalm could beat Smith if they could take and split the vote sufficiently with McCarthy's strong body of support among the Socred old guard.

When Grace McCarthy had entered the leadership race, she, like almost everyone else, had not really expected Vander Zalm to run, though she had urged him on. "We had two or three nice chats about it. I just simply encouraged him because I felt he had something to offer. And I thought it would be good to have him in the race."

In this surprising fashion, Bill Vander Zalm became the twelfth and final candidate for the leadership of the Social Credit Party.

After his news conference, Vander Zalm met with Giordano and a few other key supporters. "What do we do now?" he asked them.

Bill Vander Zalm's candidacy provoked a negative response from those prominent Socreds who saw him as a renegade they could never serve alongside. Indeed, Bill Ritchie accused Vander

Zalm of deserting the party in 1983: "It was not a time to be on the outside looking in, but on the inside looking out." Jim Nielsen was also upset with his former cabinet colleague's failure to run in the tough 1983 election and said he would have difficulty serving in a cabinet with Vander Zalm as premier: "It's not unlike the defensive line of the football team getting a little ticked off with the wide receiver who is out there and never gets his uniform dirty." Stephen Rogers stated publicly that he would not serve in a cabinet under Vander Zalm, and he offered explicit criticisms of his rival's style: "So much of his policy is the very last thing that anybody said to him, whether it was a cab driver or somebody he talked to in the hallway. I can recall being in cabinet with him when there was just no consistency."

Such comments were of greater concern to Grace McCarthy than they were to Bill Vander Zalm. Her chance of winning the leadership was dependent upon her ability to gain the support of rival candidates, but those chances were diminished by the presumption of an alliance with Vander Zalm. This put McCarthy in an extremely difficult position.

> I had a lot of pressure from my colleagues who were running. They were really upset because they kept thinking that we were a pair, that we had run on purpose together. That wasn't true. Several of them said to me: "I won't serve under this leader. If he becomes the leader I won't serve under him. And Grace, you're in cahoots with him, so I can't back you. I can't back you because you're a friend of Bill Vander Zalm."
>
> I said: "Well, you want me to go against my friendship and my loyalty to a friend, who I frankly think is a very good person. You want me to go against that in order to please you, so you'll support me. I'm sorry, I can't do that."
>
> These were the kinds of conversations I had. And they were very tough conversations. This strong feeling was so evident. And it was so sad, because I was supportive of him being in the race and supportive of him being a contender and supportive of him as an ex-colleague. And I couldn't understand why people put the responsibility on me.

Of all the candidates, Vander Zalm's campaign was the most difficult to read. He was an acknowledged front runner, but no one

was certain if the fervour he seemed to inspire amongst his followers could be translated into delegate support. Only three
Socred MLAs backed Vander Zalm: two from his political home
base of Surrey, Rita Johnston and Bill Reid, and the independent
Socred backbencher Jack Davis.

Vander Zalm was determined not to spend a lot of money on his
leadership campaign, and a distinguishing feature of his organization was that it was made up completely of volunteers, with no
paid professionals, no expensive commissioned polls and no fancy
computerized delegate tracking systems. If the Smiths' campaigns
were high-tech and Grace McCarthy's was anti-tech, then Bill
Vander Zalm's was no-tech. His campaign was based upon his personality and his magnetism, and on the spirit of old-fashioned
populism with a personal touch, and he quickly rediscovered his
magic touch with the grassroots of the Social Credit Party. (The
only visible indication that he was paying attention to the television age of political campaigning was that he trimmed his lengthy
sideburns in favour of a more modern look.) His team placed small
advertisements in newspapers throughout the province asking for
support. The response was a tidal wave of small donations. "We
were just overwhelmed with the letters that came in," recalled
Rita Johnston. "You could tell a lot of them were from people who
didn't have a lot of money. They'd send in $5 and $10. They were
just delighted to be part of his campaign for the leadership."

Charlie Giordano and Bill Goldie, from the B.C. Chamber of
Commerce, became Vander Zalm's campaign co-chairmen. Giordano said:

People just came out of the woodwork. They were phoning me at
home. And they were driving Bill crazy. And he would say: "Keep
all those telephone messages, Charlie! Keep all those cards! Keep
all those message slips!" And every day he would hand me a great
big pile of letters and messages. I would say: "Bill, what are we
going to do with them?"

"Well, weed through them, Charlie."

He used to mark right on them: "Will help." "Wants to make a
donation." "Has a problem with his coffee plant." And I'd say,
"What's this doing in here?"

He'd come into the campaign office smoking his pipe and he'd
have an old orange juice box, cut in half, with all his files and letters

in it. I'd say: "Bill, haven't you got a briefcase?"

"Oh, I like this box. It's just perfect."

But it was just too much to see this guy all dressed up, packing this old orange juice box, with all his papers in it. And he'd give me another pile.

So we'd go through all of his stuff and we'd separate the messages and phone people. But what happened was, there were so many, and the phones would keep ringing, and they would get mad because you couldn't respond to them all. We couldn't possibly respond to all these people.

With so little time to mount an effective campaign, it was a disorganized, chaotic and thrilling few weeks for Vander Zalm's fiercely partisan supporters. "People were there because they were dedicated to Bill V," said organizer Roberta Kelly. Allen Robertson, one of Vander Zalm's backroom policy advisers, suggested that "W. A. C. Bennett was Social Credit leader by *design;* Bill Bennett was leader by *default;* but Bill Vander Zalm would become leader by *desire.*"

If this was to be true, then Vander Zalm's desire expressed itself in a remarkably free-and-easy fashion. He could sense strong support from the general public but did not know if he could win it by the delegates. Nevertheless, he felt it was an easy campaign. "Regardless of what the outcome was, I would win. I couldn't lose," he said, referring to the tremendous publicity that he gained for his Fantasy Gardens theme park. Throughout the leadership campaign, Bill and Lillian Vander Zalm plugged Fantasy Gardens wherever they went. References to their burgeoning tourist attraction always found their way into Vander Zalm's speeches, and the news media often played up his involvement in his business.

(When Vander Zalm joined the leadership race he had transferred his ownership in Fantasy Gardens to his wife. The business and its complicated financing arrangements would have to be restructured to the satisfaction of the project's bankers. In addition, a pending application to have some property removed from the agricultural land reserve posed a potential conflict of interest for the gardener-who-would-be-premier. The issues were complex enough that the Vander Zalms seriously considered selling the project they had poured their dreams into.)

There was another notable difference between Bill Vander

Zalm's leadership campaign and those of the other contenders for the Socred crown. The Vander Zalm organization did not talk to the other camps. Virtually all of the other campaigns had put together sensitive communications networks geared towards identifying the slightest hints of who wanted to talk to whom about what. Candidates' agents and behind-the-scenes power brokers were in frequent touch with one another, discussing possible strategies and potential deals. The Vander Zalm people, on the other hand, kept to themselves, courting delegates and focussing solely on the goal of balloting day. This single-mindedness was misinterpreted by some as arrogance and by others as a religious zeal not to have any truck or trade with the enemy camps. Rather, it was an unpreparedness to deal with the other candidates on their own terms. For example, only a week before the convention John Laschinger returned a phone call from the Vander Zalm camp; the person who answered the phone at Vander Zalm's headquarters had never heard of Laschinger.

There were many controversies on the way to Whistler. The party struggled with the issue of campaign spending limits, deciding against implementation of rules that could not be easily enforced. Still, the money spent by the candidates for the Socred leadership was a major issue by the time they got to Whistler. It was estimated that collectively more cash was spent than the party had expended during the last general election campaign—two to three million dollars. Some candidates did not even have budgets; they simply spent. The political debts would be collected later.

Perhaps the most controversial issue, vividly indicating the key rifts in the Social Credit family, was the public revelation of the Top 20. Leadership candidates were invited to a series of luncheons with this confidential fundraising arm of the party, but Grace McCarthy refused to appear before what Vancouver *Sun* columnist Marjorie Nichols referred to as a "closed-door strip search." McCarthy was soon joined by Bill Vander Zalm, who bolstered her view that special power groups like the Top 20 were antidemocratic. McCarthy and Vander Zalm, espousing traditional Social Credit populism, argued that the clandestine business group was an example of how the party had drifted from its grassroots into the grip of power brokers who were supporting Bud and Brian Smith. Vander Zalm regretted that Social Credit had become "the party of Howe Street," and he promised to change that. Meanwhile, the fifty-eight businessmen who made up the Top 20 were named in the news media. (See Appendix.) Mike Burns later suggested that Grace McCarthy had taken "this particular piece of the party and used it as a battering ram for her campaign." Burns believed it was an indication of "a scorched earth leadership campaign."

In spite of the posturing over special interest groups, all candidates knew it was only the delegates who would select the new Social Credit leader. Thirteen hundred were elected to vote at Whistler: 431 from the Greater Vancouver area; 292 from the southern Interior; 235 each from Vancouver Island and the north, and 117 from the Fraser Valley. Each constituency, even dual-member ridings, sent twenty-five delegates—a contentious aspect of the delegate selection process that penalized candidates such as Grace McCarthy, whose base of support, the lower mainland's populous urban ridings, was under-represented. Most candidates could count on strength from a single geographic region; only Bill Vander Zalm appeared to have a basis of support in all parts of the province.

With his sophisticated delegate tracking system, John Laschinger learned that the average age of the delegates was forty-seven, and one-third of them were women. Their average annual family income was $39,000. And the average length of membership in the party was 12.4 years—the average delegate voting at Whistler had been a party member during W. A. C. Bennett's tenure as leader.

Laschinger's data also revealed that "the party out here is further to the right than any place I've seen." "Lasch" used an ideological spectrum of one to ten, with one being left and ten being right. He said: "The average of the Conservative Party federally is about 5.4 to 5.5, and they perceived Mulroney to be about 5.7 to 5.8, Joe Clark was 5—right in the middle, John Crosbie was 5.6." But in British Columbia, Laschinger discovered that the average Socred saw himself as a 6.6 to 6.7. The Socreds saw Vander Zalm at 7.5; Grace McCarthy at 6.9, Bud Smith and Brian Smith at 6.4. "A good chunk of them felt that the party would have to move to the centre to win an election," he said. "But they wanted to govern back on the right. They were very sophisticated."

Although a populist political culture will always distrust public opinion polls, the Whistler experience only reconfirmed their value. Polls rarely lie, and as the leadership race approached the climax of the convention, they were all saying the same thing. Laschinger conducted his last poll two and a half weeks before the convention started. "It was all over," he said. "Vander Zalm was going to win it on the third or fourth ballot."

No one wanted to believe this evidence, but clearly Vander Zalm's campaign had the other candidates spooked. His personal appeal and charisma were overwhelming. Even the news media were falling over themselves to capture a glimpse of the smiling Vander Zalms and their energetic campaign. "The race was over in my view about ten days before Whistler," said Patrick Kinsella. "Vander Zalm had an event at Fantasy Gardens, and BCTV ran it as their top story. It was six minutes of television time. There are certain things you cannot ignore. It was a love-in."

Laschinger's and Kinsella's private perspectives became public knowledge when, the Saturday prior to the leadership convention, the Vancouver *Sun* published the results of a specially commissioned poll as its front-page headline story. The poll canvassed the public province-wide and found that Vander Zalm led all other candidates in every category of question asked. Fifty per cent of British Columbians thought Vander Zalm would be best at providing strong leadership; Grace McCarthy was a distant second with 16.9 per cent. Vander Zalm was considered the best candidate to end confrontation in British Columbia; McCarthy was a distant second. Vander Zalm would best represent British Columbia's interests outside the province; McCarthy was far back in second place. Vander Zalm was the most trusted leader; McCarthy was in second place. And fully 50.2 per cent believed that Vander Zalm had the best chance of winning the next election. Then, as the convention opened on Monday, BCTV broadcast the results of its own public opinion poll, showing that almost 50 per cent of British Columbians would like to see Vander Zalm as the next Social Credit leader; Grace McCarthy trailed with 20 per cent support; all other candidates were far, far behind.

These widely discussed polls shaped the moods and attitudes of the candidates, their organizers, the delegates, the media and the many hangers-on who made the trek to Whistler for three exhilarating days of politics, politics and more politics. Few believed that a Vander Zalm victory was inevitable. For most of the foot soldiers in the leadership battle, he was simply the man to beat. But for others, the possibility of a Vander Zalm victory was the source of grave concern and the cause of desperate actions. In particular, Patrick Kinsella attempted to challenge the possibility of a Vander Zalm victory. On the day the convention opened, in an unprecedented move for a campaign manager, Kinsella held a rare news conference at which he claimed that a Stop Vander Zalm movement existed and that Bud Smith's support was softening, and suggested Brian Smith was the logical compromise candidate. "I set out to do that," he later said, "so that the news media would feel that Vander Zalm was home and cooled out. It looks desperate now, but the fact was that it was provocative enough to think about."

Kinsella's news conference and his vigorous attempts to set the agenda for the convention backfired. Most significantly, his efforts seriously diminished the chances of a Smith/Smith alliance. In the week leading up to Whistler, the Brian Smith and Bud Smith camps had an understanding that their candidates were vying for third or fourth spot on the first ballot. They also had a tacit agreement that whichever candidate finished fourth on the first ballot would support the one who finished third. Kinsella's news conference sparked an aggressive word-of-mouth campaign by the Brian Smith camp alleging that Bud Smith's support was sliding. Such tactics upset many Bud Smith supporters. Peter Hyndman, Bud Smith's campaign co-chairman, later said: "We didn't feel nearly so wonderful about the Brian Smith organization as we did a few days earlier."

So with the "Smith Bros." alliance in a fragile state and all other pacts, real or imagined, in limbo, on Monday, 28 July 1986 the Social Credit leadership convention commenced.

Of the leading contenders, Bill Vander Zalm's campaign was the least ostentatious. Aside from his tent on the golf course, there were no visible signs of extravagance. This was in part because of his late entry into the race: all of the hotels, restaurants and watering-holes at Whistler had already been booked. But Bill and Lillian Vander Zalm walked through the village each evening, talking and joking and dancing with delegates, always attracting a throng of followers, always the centre of attention. Said one delegate: "They're just like the Kennedys."

The rumour-mills worked twenty-four hours a day. The combination of financial difficulties and lack of delegate support led to suggestions that some candidates might withdraw from the race before the balloting began. Imagined or hoped-for alliances, leaked public opinion polls, delegate switching, arm twisting—all of the hype normally associated with these contests was in ample evidence. And humour too. One candidate referred to rival Bob Wenman, a Christian fundamentalist: "He's going to be a very disappointed man the first Easter after he dies." Of Grace McCarthy's Operation Grassroots campaign, one overly impressed opponent said: "It sure takes a lot of money to represent the grassroots." And a Brian Smith supporter, upset with Finance Minister Hugh Curtis's last-minute endorsement of Grace McCarthy, said: "On a pomposity scale of one to ten, Hugh's a fourteen." Graham Lea, attending the convention as a media representative, was asked to compare this contest with the 1984 NDP leadership convention, in which he had been a candidate: "Here the women shave their legs."

John Laschinger, who had attended several leadership conventions throughout Canada, said that all such conventions are different: "There's no rule. The only thing for certain is you can always expect the unexpected." At Whistler, a special intensity underlay both the deliberations and the festivities. Many of the delegates declared this to be the most thrilling and emotional time of their lives, and accordingly they took their roles seriously—far more than observers gave them credit for. Delegates approached the Whistler experience with a kind of religious zeal which suggested something more than the normal, healthy competition among rival family members. After all, choosing a new leader was serious business. Close observers, sensitive to British Columbia's populist tradition, may have caught a scent of protest—if not redress—in the mountain air.

The first day of the convention was devoted to organization, registration, orientation and getting the party started. Amongst the plentiful and fanciful rumours of deals and alliances was the revelation that Grace McCarthy was being assisted by Kirk Foley, who had worked with the Big Blue Machine. McCarthy, who had campaigned vigorously against the machine politics and out-of-province political professionals of the Smith forces, was now forced to defend her own.

The issue of British Columbia citizenship was one of the underlying themes of the leadership race. James Coleridge, a young McCarthy organizer, said it was "unfortunate that the Rocky Mountains aren't tall enough to prevent the planes from flying over from the east." And at Whistler it was evident that many Socreds would never be able to surmount these mental Rockies. The Vancouver *Sun*'s schizophrenic editorial endorsement of both Grace McCarthy and Brian Smith as "the two best for premier" was used as part of the promotional package of both candidates' camps. But when the Toronto *Globe and Mail* offered its endorsement of Bud Smith as the best hope for B.C. renewal, it was derided as the "kiss of death." Brian Smith's organization, in a further attempt to discredit Bud Smith, went so far as to print and circulate hundreds of copies of the *Globe*'s editorial.

The highlight of the convention's opening day was an evening tribute and emotional farewell to the retiring leader, Premier Bill Bennett. In his valedictory address, Bennett took one last opportunity to tell his party that "Social Credit is not a coalition." He also spoke of renewal, but even more strongly emphasized unity. Touching lightly on suggestions that the succession of leadership had damaged Social Credit, Bennett said: "I know it will heal, just as it healed after 1973."

Tuesday, 29 July, following a long evening of partying, revelry and rivalry, was devoted to policy sessions throughout the day and candidates' keynote addresses in the evening. It was a day of shopping the candidates before the delegates, firming up the undecided and struggling for first ballot support. Rotating policy sessions on the topics of leadership, the economy and social policy filled the afternoon with energetic campaigning and hoopla, but there were few new ideas or pronouncements on policy. Clearly, Whistler was foremost a personality contest.

Most candidates believed that their addresses would fire up their own supporters and obtain last-minute delegate support; many of them felt that these would be among the most important speeches of their careers. Some rose to the occasion; some did not.

The order of speakers had been chosen by lot a few days earlier, and first up was Jim Nielsen, whose speech contained strong hints of desperation and bitterness. "There are no backroom boys making my decisions for me," he said, "or even cutting my sideburns." In a populist and paranoid flourish, Nielsen told the attentive delegates: "Look around you. Powerful forces are at work here. Powerful forces are at work to influence you. And deals have been struck. But who speaks for you?"

Cabinet minister Bill Ritchie's blustery speech was followed by Conservative MP Bob Wenman's. He quoted W. A. C. Bennett: "To central Canada, British Columbia is just a goblet to be drained. We're going to take the goblet back to Ottawa and say, 'Fill it up!' "

Bud Smith, the only candidate to make a pointed effort to align himself with the outgoing leader, was also the only contender who had never held elected office. The former principal secretary to Premier Bennett brushed away criticisms with the assertion that "the only experience that counts is the experience of serving the office itself."

Cliff Michael, though given little chance of making it beyond the first ballot, delivered a spirited address pleading with the delegates: "I ask you to give all these reporters something to write about." Mel Couvelier, defying Bill Bennett's definition, described Social Credit as a "coalition of free enterprisers." The Liberal mayor said of the leadership succession: "We cannot put the past through a photocopy machine and call it the present." Meanwhile, Stephen Rogers, the self-styled dark horse candidate, offered a dull, almost indifferent oration, causing many delegates to wonder why he was in the race.

Before the evening had a chance to sag, Grace McCarthy was on stage launching into an effective appeal to Social Credit traditions. Describing herself as a "positive thinker" and a "possibility thinker," she stated: "We do not reserve places for the influential few. That's not my style." She referred to the "deliverances from disaster" of the past, such as 1952 when W. A. C. defeated "corrupt political machines that degraded this magnificent province." She spoke of 1975 when the Social Credit Party regained power, thanks in large part to her own organizational prowess. "My friends," said McCarthy, using a familiar W. A. C. Bennett-ism, "we've done it before and we'll do it again."

John Reynolds, the host-MLA at Whistler, was followed by Kim Campbell, who delivered perhaps the most memorable speech of the long evening. The tenth candidate to address the wilting crowd, Campbell had surprised many Socreds by even making it as far as Whistler, so prevalent were rumours that she would withdraw from the race for lack of support. Now, by the luck of the draw, her well-considered remarks were broadcast on prime-time television, raising Social Credit's credibility with a wide audience. She criticized the NDP for their "politics of envy" and distrust of success. She also delivered a line which appeared to be a direct shot at Bill Vander Zalm: "Charisma without substance is a dangerous thing." This would echo throughout the convention and beyond, becoming a clarion call for the next generation of west coast political activists.

Attorney General Brian Smith's floor demonstration was a slickly choreographed affair replete with a laser light show and his speech was probably the best one of his career. Immediately following his claim that he had single-handedly solved the prostitution problem in Vancouver's west end, he promised: "I'll be a hands on premier, I'll tell you. . . . But not in the west end."

Bill Vander Zalm had the last word on this long, exhausting evening. In the final ten days of the campaign Vander Zalm and his organization had urged delegates for their support on the first ballot. The Vander Zalm camp was worried because their own informal canvassing of delegates indicated that their candidate was a popular second choice. However, their vigorous campaigning, combined with Vander Zalm's magnetic appeal, and buoyed by the results of published polls, made for a set of circumstances that was less than desperate.

The consummate campaigner climbed onto the stage with his family to the accompaniment of his driving campaign song, composed and sung by his daughter Juanita. "It's great to be back," proclaimed Vander Zalm to a sea of waving pink placards. His address was less rousing than many expected. In a separatist flourish, he attacked central Canada for its dominance within confederation and for holding back western and B.C. development. Turning to the campaign of the moment, he said: "I have made no deals with anyone—not the other candidates and not their consultants. I won't be making any deals with anyone. A cabinet post or a consulting job won't be traded. It must be earned." Then he made the most direct and astonishing appeal to the delegates of any of the candidates that evening. He reminded the assembled Socreds that in 1973, Bill Bennett had won the leadership convention on the first ballot. Bennett had said that if he had not been victorious, it could have been the start of an anybody-but-Bill movement.

Vander Zalm warned: "Another Bill, thirteen years later, could be faced with the same problem. This Bill needs your support on the first ballot."

The remainder of this restless night was given to partying, rallying the troops and assessing the speeches. There were also many attempts at deal-making and alliances for the following day of voting; there were many handshakes on deals that would never be completed. Meanwhile, Bill Vander Zalm had a late dinner with his wife and closest advisers at their hotel headquarters. During dinner, Vander Zalm called for their attention and whispered: "I just want everyone to know and understand—there are no deals."

Early the next morning, groggy and hung-over campaign workers filed into the convention centre to prepare for battle. With the garish colours, the wild banners and the blaring music, the adrenalin soon started to flow. Everyone acknowledged that this was likely to be a long, hot day. And everyone was prepared to be surprised.

While the finishing touches were being placed on the faces of the campaigns in the convention centre, all of the dozen leadership hopefuls were having a private breakfast with the retiring leader. The twelve apostles were not all disciples of this leader, but they accepted his invitation for breakfast and listened to his plea for unity. The premier asked each of the candidates to take responsibility for their most fervent and emotional supporters—to prevent them from doing or saying anything that could hurt or damage the Social Credit Party. He also asked them to show solidarity behind the new leader. They all agreed and pledged unity.

When convention chairman Les Peterson opened the balloting at 10:30 A.M., half an hour late, all twelve candidates' names were still on the ballot. It would take almost two hours for the delegates to cast their votes and for the results to be tabulated and announced. Meanwhile, the floor demonstrations were waged with military force against the cacophony of the leading candidates' campaign songs. And in the background a lot of discussion took place—last-minute poking and prodding at the assumed strengths and weaknesses of the various contenders' camps.

The agony of this first long wait of the day came to an end shortly after noon when Les Peterson read the results to the momentarily hushed hall. Vander Zalm was on top with 367 votes, well short of his personal prediction. Grace McCarthy followed with 244. Bud

Smith was in third spot with 202, and Brian Smith was in a close fourth with 196. The Caucus Five reeled in horror as Jim Nielsen and John Reynolds tied at 54 apiece. Stephen Rogers was next with 43; Bob Wenman had 40; Cliff Michael 32; Bill Ritchie 28. Mel Couvelier finished with 20 and Kim Campbell was in last place with 14 votes.

Vander Zalm, in the lead but a long way from victory, later recalled: "I thought I would pull heavier than what I did on the first ballot. I was out by a good 20 to 25 per cent." McCarthy had also hoped for a stronger showing for herself. The Smiths were too close to call, though Brian Smith and his handler, Patrick Kinsella, lost some face over their boasts of being well ahead of Bud Smith. These four leading candidates captured 78 per cent of the total vote while the other eight contenders lost their $2,500 deposits as a consequence of not receiving the required 100 votes. Total delegate support for the noncaucus candidates nearly equalled that of the elected Social Credit contenders. The urge for party renewal was strongly evident.

There was no assured victory for anyone in these numbers. Vander Zalm declared: "We're going to have to work all the harder now." Although it was impossible to know if candidates could deliver their delegates to a rival by joining their platform, the emotions of the convention could undoubtedly be influenced by the *appearance* of movement. The outcome of the convention could be decided quickly if the correct movements took place—that is, if the handshakes and promises held.

Kim Campbell, the last-place finisher, moved quickly to Brian Smith. Mel Couvelier, who it was said had shaken hands on a deal with Brian Smith, moved to Vander Zalm. The tie between Reynolds and Nielsen was enough to crack the fragile coalition of the Caucus Five. Rogers indicated that he was going to Brian Smith. Ritchie would follow. Cliff Michael, in what became a futile move, decided to go with Reynolds. Both Reynolds and Nielsen would stay on for the second ballot.

In a move that devastated the McCarthy camp, Bob Wenman then joined Brian Smith. The Conservative MP said: "It was strictly a matter of numbers. And it seemed clear to me that others weren't going to her. The movement seemed to be to Brian. It was a difficult decision because my heart was with Grace." His rationalization was utterly lost on Grace McCarthy, the godmother of one of Wenman's children. The McCarthy camp had been told to prepare to greet Wenman with open arms. His decision, and Stephen Rogers's and, later, Jim Nielsen's, were strongly influenced by the perception that McCarthy would ultimately support Vander Zalm. Thus, in a strange turn of events, Amazing Grace was harmed by a latent Stop Vander Zalm movement, not receiving the endorsement of a single rival candidate.

Most of the movement seemed to be going to Brian Smith. An excited Patrick Kinsella appeared live on CBC television: "Bill Vander Zalm has got to be devastated by what happened. He predicted 550 on the first ballot. . . . Where does he grow? How does he grow? I think the growth is us. I think the growth is coming from all those people who have jammed up on our stage. Brian may be a compromise candidate, but he's going to be the next premier of the province."

Of course, Kinsella had hoped that Brian Smith would finish in third spot and that Bud Smith would then come quickly to their side. Bud Smith's handlers now found out that this hoped-for arrangement was by no means reciprocal. And this would help influence Bud Smith's ultimate move. But for now it was simply too close, and it appeared that Brian Smith had the momentum.

Only half a dozen names remained on the second ballot. Behind the scenes, while the delegates voted once more, campaign managers negotiated furiously. The general expectation remained that if Brian Smith moved ahead of Bud Smith, as was now likely, then Bud would throw his support to Brian. Vander Zalm declared: "If the Smiths coalesced and got it together, then I would be talking to Grace and she would be talking to me." Meanwhile, Jim Nielsen indicated to McCarthy that he wanted to see the results of the second ballot before deciding what to do. Then McCarthy held a prearranged meeting with opponent Bud Smith. The five-minute get-together was not constructive and crystallized Bud's decision to make a dramatic move elsewhere. Charlie Giordano, a Vander Zalm floor organizer, had made some contact with Bud Smith's camp. He now asked Vander Zalm for permission to approach Bud Smith personally. But Vander Zalm was hesitant, saying: "No deals. Please, Charlie, don't offer anything."

Everywhere in the convention centre people were tugging on loyalties, emotions and personalities. The boisterous mood on the convention floor contrasted the backroom view seen by only a few.

In small meeting rooms in the convention centre basement, candidates, campaign managers, strategists and others privately negotiated for support. Asked for and offered were cabinet posts, liquidation of campaign debts, and jobs for key supporters. If any such deals were struck, there is no evidence that they influenced the day's events.

Perhaps the most talked-about backroom activity was later associated with the Vander Zalm campaign. This is ironic because Vander Zalm was probably the only candidate who refused to consider deals of any kind. However, his campaign was made up largely of enthusiastic amateurs who, though well-meaning, created deep, lasting controversies.

Peter Toigo, Vander Zalm's friend and business adviser, came to Whistler to help out and ended up becoming a key campaign organizer, convention floor worker and power broker. Said Toigo: "I found myself a negotiator with all these people without even knowing what I was doing." Toigo coincidentally operated the kitchen facilities in the Whistler convention centre. In a small office in the basement, adjacent to the kitchen, he held court with a special guest who had flown into Whistler for the day. This was the chairman of the Bank of British Columbia, Edgar Kaiser Jr.

Kaiser's presence at Whistler was difficult to conceal, especially when he emerged from the basement to wander around the convention floor. Later it was suggested that the wealthy and controversial Kaiser had come to influence the contest by offering to pay off the campaign debts of candidates who crossed the floor to Bill Vander Zalm. Other wild and unsubstantiated rumours circulated about Kaiser trying to buy a government.

A bit of a political junkie, Kaiser was both fascinated by the political process and interested in its outcome. As chairman of the struggling Bank of B.C., Kaiser was also having extreme difficulty in securing the co-operation and support of the provincial government. He believed the change in leadership might provide an opportunity for a stronger commitment from Victoria for the regional bank's continued survival. He met with Vander Zalm prior to Whistler and became supportive of his views and of his candidacy. He said that he did not in any direct way support Vander Zalm financially.

Toigo later accepted the responsibility for inviting Edgar Kaiser to Whistler on the day of the vote. Toigo believed that Brian Smith

would be Vander Zalm's strongest opponent and knew that Kaiser
was a friend of Patrick Kinsella's. "We felt that Kaiser could help
deliver Brian Smith," Toigo said. In Toigo's view, the invitation
to Kaiser almost backfired when Kinsella attempted to persuade
Kaiser that Brian Smith would win the day and that supporting
Brian was the only logical thing to do. Kaiser also regretted going
to Whistler because the effect of his attendance was, in his view,
later blown out of proportion by the news media.

In any event, several candidates and campaign managers did
meet with Peter Toigo and Edgar Kaiser, generally being escorted
to the kitchen meeting room via a special elevator directly behind
Grace McCarthy's campaign platform. Toigo and Kaiser urged the
candidates or their representatives to support Vander Zalm. But
they had no luck with Patrick Kinsella who argued that Bud Smith
was coming over to Brian Smith who was going to win the day. And
so here was Edgar Kaiser, not a Social Credit Party member, but
wanting to back the winner of the contest, and Peter Toigo, a political novice, trying to match wits and negotiate with political professionals. "It was the most exciting day I ever had," recalled
Toigo.

The results of the second ballot, announced at 3:30 P.M., surprised many observers. Vander Zalm gained 90 votes to increase
his lead to 457. McCarthy, in spite of the complete lack of candidate movement to her, showed no slippage; she increased her total
to 280. Brian Smith was now in third place with 255. Bud Smith
also gained supporters but had dropped into fourth spot with 219.
Reynolds finished with 39 and Nielsen with 30.

The pace immediately quickened. Bill Vander Zalm exclaimed:
"That's great! Gracie's made advances, too, so we'll have to see
what happens." In the McCarthy camp there were cheers of jubilation over the fact that they had made gains and held onto second
place. The ballot results showed the independence of the Socred
delegates and proved that most candidates could deliver only a por-
tion of their delegates to another camp. All of the support that
seemed headed towards Brian Smith could not catapult him into
second spot—delegates were going their own way.

John Reynolds now moved quickly to Vander Zalm, followed
closely by Cliff Michael, carrying Vander Zalm's political emblem,
a golden shovel. A swarm of Vander Zalm floor workers surged towards the McCarthy camp carrying a sea of pink placards and pink

flamingos. "Bill wants Grace! Bill wants Grace!" they chanted. But McCarthy was not budging and still looked for movement to her platform.

Meanwhile, Jim Nielsen decided to go to Brian Smith where the majority of his cabinet colleagues had congregated. One more disappointment for McCarthy. The Brian Smith organization remained hopeful that Bud would come their way; Grace McCarthy's camp was also waiting desperately to see what he would do.

Bud Smith decided to acquiesce to the will of the convention and make a move that he had discussed only with his wife. It was later suggested that Bud first consulted with Bill Bennett before making his decision. The premier denied this but later endorsed Bud's decision as the correct move considering the mood of the delegates. In his headquarters adjacent to the convention centre, Bud Smith rallied his advisers and key strategists, offered a quick analysis of the situation and revealed his decision to cross the floor to Bill Vander Zalm.

"For a few seconds we were all really surprised," said Peter Hyndman. "And then it seemed to make a lot of sense given how the day was developing." The one option that virtually no one could have predicted was about to be played out, the most dramatic moment in a day filled with drama. With only moments to spare, Bud Smith and his team quickly made their way back to the convention centre to officially withdraw from the next ballot and, they hoped, push Vander Zalm over the top.

Bud Smith made his way through the crush of delegates and curious reporters, back to his stage in the convention centre. As he climbed onto his platform, convention chairman Les Peterson announced that his name would be dropped from the third ballot. In the heat of the moment, different observers saw different events. Bud Smith's platform was immediately adjacent to Brian Smith's, where organizers were preparing to make room for Bud and his people. The noise, the crowd and the pressure made for a special brand of chaos. Some observers claimed that Patrick Kinsella shouted over to Bud Smith: "We need you now!" The same persons claim that Bud responded to Kinsella by mouthing the words: "You're dead!"

Less dramatic is Kinsella's version:

I was trying to get Bud's attention. He was standing on a chair in his platform and I caught his eye. I said: "Bud, we need you." He shook his head. He said nothing. But he looked truly sad. He left his platform. I turned to Tom Waterland and asked: "Where's he going?" Tom said: "There's no stopping Vander Zalm." I said: "What? He can't be going there!" Waterland repeated: "There's no stopping Vander Zalm."

Bud Smith does not think Pat Kinsella caught his eye. Bud tried to call Vander Zalm on the convention centre's communication system to tell him of his decision, but the phone was out of order. A few key Vander Zalm organizers were in touch with Bud Smith's people and had an idea of what was about to happen. Bud and his wife, Daphne, with some close supporters forming an arm-lock around them, began to make their way across the hall.

With the placards waving and the floor demonstrations converging on the centre of the hall, it was impossible for anyone to see exactly what was happening. As Bud Smith's group shifted to one side to make their way through the crowd, some thought he was turning to Brian Smith's stage. Across the hall Vander Zalm strained to see what was happening. Charlie Giordano had advised Vander Zalm that Bud Smith was coming over. Now Vander Zalm said to Giordano: "He's going to Brian." Giordano said: "No, he's coming to us." But the Vander Zalm floor organizer thought to himself: "Maybe he *is* going to Brian Smith. Has he betrayed us?" As Bud Smith and his party worked their way across the hall, many McCarthy supporters believed they were coming to Grace's platform.

It was shortly after four o'clock when Bud Smith climbed onto Vander Zalm's stage and shook hands with a beaming Vander Zalm who hugged Smith, who in turn was stiff with a look of discomfort and a tight smile. Vander Zalm exclaimed: "Fantastic . . . maybe it's three now." Bud Smith declared: "The delegates wanted renewal. And I thought I represented that. Mr. Vander Zalm represents that."

The reaction on the convention floor was one of confusion, surprise and shock. There would be only three names on the third, and perhaps last, ballot. A disappointed Grace McCarthy said: "It's confusing, isn't it?" Patrick Kinsella remarked: "I'm absolutely shocked. Totally stunned." "He said he'd never go there," said bewildered cabinet minister Claude Richmond. Vander Zalm organizer Bill Goldie said: "It was never considered that he would be the one to make the move. I thought Grace McCarthy would be the one to make the move."

As delegates queued to vote for a third time, everyone wondered if Bud Smith could deliver his surprised, ill-prepared supporters to guarantee a quick Vander Zalm victory. And now, too late, the Brian Smith camp began to push, prod and cajole Grace Mc-Carthy's people into an alliance to stop Vander Zalm. She was, however, resolute, saying: "I'm not putting my support to them. . . . I'm not comfortable going to them. The next ballot will be either Brian Smith against Bill Vander Zalm or Grace McCarthy and Bill Vander Zalm."

While awaiting the third ballot results there was a great deal of frantic dialogue between the Brian Smith and Grace McCarthy camps. An understanding seemed to develop that if Vander Zalm fell short of a victory and McCarthy was still in second place, Brian Smith and the cabinet coalition would move to Grace for a final and decisive ballot. However, if Brian Smith was in second spot, McCarthy agreed only to release her delegates to vote with their consciences.

At six o'clock the results of the third ballot were announced. Bill Vander Zalm 625—12 votes short of a victory. Brian Smith 342. Grace McCarthy 305.

The immediate reaction on Brian Smith's packed platform was jubilation; it would take some time for the realization and panic of defeat to set in. On McCarthy's stage there was an outburst of emotion. "That's it," said Ray McCarthy, Grace's husband. McCarthy leaned over to her campaign worker John Plul and asked him to ensure that all her delegates were immediately informed that they should vote their consciences on the next ballot. Cabinet ministers and staunch McCarthy loyalists Pat McGeer, Garde Gardom, Elwood Veitch and Hugh Curtis shook hands, resigning themselves and their fates to the convention. A tower of strength, McCarthy embraced her tearful campaign workers. "Come on, you guys," she said, "don't be so sentimental."

Ironically, McCarthy was probably the candidate with the greatest ability to "deliver" her delegates wherever she wished, so strong was the loyalty she inspired in her troops. And yet she was the only candidate that day to drop off the ballot without formally endorsing another contender. She had no need to do so. She could not and would not willingly support the Brian Smith machine and Patrick Kinsella. Knowing how her people would vote and that her own campaign was over, she could easily resolve herself to the now imminent victory of her "dear enemy," Bill Vander Zalm.

However, McCarthy would not move to Vander Zalm's platform. A small core of her supporters could not support him, and she would not offend or shun them now; she did not wish to let anyone down. "That day I was able to walk out of there feeling I had done my best for everybody," she said later. "And I don't have to make a point with Bill Vander Zalm. My people were basically his people and his people were my people." Some of Vander Zalm's more strident supporters were extremely upset with McCarthy's decision to retire from the race without demonstrating solidarity with their candidate. "I had gone through a very exhausting time," recalled McCarthy, "and I just needed to get out of the hall. It was obvious where it was going to go. I cast my vote for him and then I went back to see the end result."

An effort was made to eliminate the need for a fourth ballot with the suggestion that Brian Smith should concede defeat, parade over to Vander Zalm's platform and stage a joint procession to the stage. Smith refused, while his workers made a futile effort to have Grace McCarthy come over to him. "You know you can't win," Kinsella told Brian Smith. "Yes, I know," he replied. However, like McCarthy he was both proud and determined to follow, not lead, his supporters. "If the delegates to this convention want Bill Vander Zalm as their premier," said the attorney general, "then they'll have to elect him." For his part, Vander Zalm was supremely patient. "It just means we'll have to sit here for another two hours," he said, "but I feel marvellous. The process works. It goes to show that the machines can't do it. The grassroots has spoken."

The need for a fourth ballot allowed the Social Credit convention to compose itself. Pride, ego and desire to let the marathon run its course prevented a variety of efforts to show party solidarity before the fourth ballot results were announced. However, the pandemonium of the day's events settled into an inchoate understanding that this was a day of protest for a dynamic, populist party. If Vander Zalm had won on the third ballot, following Bud Smith's remarkable move, the convention would have ended in chaos. Now, between the third and fourth ballots, Bud Smith was able to assemble most of his campaign workers to explain his actions and to describe his sense that the goal of renewal would be served. Some of his supporters may not have agreed, but at least his accounting took some of the sting out of their earlier surprise.

At Whistler at the end of the day, on the final ballot, in the stuffy, congested convention centre, stood a paradox. Two Social Credit parties stood facing each other, waiting for the final numbers. On one side of the hall was Bill Vander Zalm and a massive crowd of supporters, mavericks like himself and others who had caved in to the force of his campaign. On the other side was Brian Smith and an amazingly complete coalition of the Socred establishment. The final vote was announced at 8:15 P.M: Vander Zalm 801; Brian Smith 454.

In an impressive display of unity, televised province-wide, the new leader and his wife, exhilarated and relieved in this anti-climactic victory, made their way through the thick, congratulating crowd as their daughter, Juanita, sang live on stage her father's rocking campaign song: "He's a growing sensation . . . Bill Vander Zalm . . . He's our man."

On the crowded stage under the glaring lights, runner-up Brian Smith gave a gracious, statesmanlike speech, in which he promised: "We will all be together, Bill." Next to speak was Grace McCarthy who was at her best and showing no signs of emotional emptiness. To a rousing ovation she said: "The NDP must be eating its heart out right now." And turning to the leader-elect, she declared: "Have we ever got a job to do in the coming months in British Columbia."

Outgoing leader Bill Bennett was on hand to pass the torch to his successor. In a brief but high-charged speech Bennett said: "I know that Bill Vander Zalm can lead this party. I know that he can run a government. I know that Bill Vander Zalm can lead and be part of a team. . . . I know he can be all of the things that British Columbia cries out for and the people of this party want. All of us should consider this one of our moments. We have a new leader with proven capabilities. A new leader with a capacity to lead us to victory."

Then, smiling but subdued, the new leader spoke. He gave his trademark adjective, "Faaantaastic!" Referring to himself, as he often did, in the third person, he said: "This is truly a very humble

and very proud moment for Bill Vander Zalm." In an unprecedented gesture for a politician, he thanked the news media "for
making the public more aware of the democratic process and the
wonders of Social Credit." In the CBC television booth, off the convention floor, media commentator Yvonne Cocke, a veteran NDP
organizer, watched the impressive display of Socred solidarity in
horror. As Vander Zalm concluded his remarks, Cocke confided off
camera: "My god, he'll eat Skelly alive."

That night in the Whistler village the victory celebrations and
losers' wakes wound their way into the warm summer night. It is
strange but true that most people who nourish themselves in the
political life are in the game not to make history but to be diverted
from the history that is being made. For many, this night was one
last diversion. For others, like Vander Zalm campaign organizer
Roberta Kelly, it was "an all-time high," though she later confessed: "If I had any feeling of a low, it was the fact that there were
people there who had worked twice as long as I had for people they
were totally committed to. There were men crying in the streets
because they really believed that their candidate was going to
come out a winner."

At Brian Smith's headquarters the music blared and the party
rolled on into the early hours of the morning. Patrick Kinsella
greeted everyone at the entrance to the bar by painting on them
long green sideburns, an obvious parody of the new party leader's
decision midway through the campaign to trim his sideburns. As
candidates, their spouses, journalists and political groupies
boogied to the rock n' roll wearing monstrous green sideburns, a
fatigued Kinsella wandered back to his hotel room muttering: "I
think I should go back to Ontario. . . ."

Meanwhile, the new leader was making the obligatory gestures
of thanks and graciously receiving the loud ovations of the partying
delegates. Surrounding Vander Zalm that night were his family,
close advisers and key campaign workers. All were savouring the
exhilaration of their triumph. Few noticed, but the new leader's
face did not reflect the same ecstasy of victory. His naturally broad
smile seemed forced; he appeared tired, concerned, pensive. It
was not exhaustion that had set in, but rather a stunned realization
that he had indeed won the party leadership and the premiership
of the province. "Now what?" he wondered.

CHAPTER 5

Changing of the Guard

For two decades Bill Vander Zalm had been a controversial public figure in British Columbia, receiving as much media attention as some premiers. But little was known of his background—the story of an immigrant boy rising to success as a businessman and politician, a story that is a tribute to Canadian democracy.

Vander Zalm's parents were prominent in the Catholic town of Noordwykerhout, in the heart of Holland's bulb-growing district; his father was a bulb salesman and a partner in the family business established by his own father before him. Young Wilhelmus, or Wim, was strongly influenced not only by his family's staunch, orthodox Catholicism but also by the other fact of Dutch life: mercantilism. The bulb trade dominated the local economy, and most families shared a resolute work ethic.

Wilhelmus Vander Zalm Sr. spent six months of every year selling bulbs in North America, leaving his wife to care for their seven children. In 1939, when war broke out, he was stranded in the New World. While he laid the groundwork for a gardening business in Bradner, in British Columbia's fertile Fraser Valley, his family in Holland struggled through the war years with little or no income. There was no heat, their mother sometimes had to beg, and they subsisted on a diet of tulip bulbs. This war-torn, fatherless and often destitute childhood demonstrated to young Bill that the virtues of faith, family and hard work could carry one through even the most trying of times.

Their father returned in the spring of 1947—when Bill was twelve—not to stay but to take his family back to Bradner. Postwar British Columbia was on the verge of rapid development, and they were exciting times. While his father built up his business, Bill attended school in Abbotsford, where he was an above-average student, a good soccer player and popular with the girls. Gradually he was assimilated into mainstream Canadian society, and in 1952, the year he graduated, he became a Canadian citizen.

Bill had considered a career in law, but had also thought about becoming a bulb salesman, for he had learned skills from his father, who could, he said, "sell refrigerators to the Eskimos. He was always positive, no matter how tough things were in the industry. We all gained this optimism. And I think we're all reasonably good salespeople in the family, from him." His decision was made for him shortly before his graduation. When his father had a heart attack, seventeen-year-old Bill was catapulted into the bulb-selling business, assuming responsibility for developing and maintaining customer accounts throughout western Canada.

In Kelowna, on one of his sales trips, he met Lillian Mihalic, a Catholic with a Yugoslavian-Ukrainian background, and they married in the summer of 1956. Theirs has always been a strong and happy partnership—to this day they behave like newlyweds—and Lillian has supported virtually all of Bill Vander Zalm's activities.

The young couple moved to Surrey and began to raise a family. Bill Vander Zalm bought Art Knapp's Nurseries Ltd. and opened several plant, shrub and gardening supply outlets. The profitable nursery business began to give Vander Zalm his trademark image of a man of the earth.

By the mid-1960s Vander Zalm was applying his Dutch work ethic and boundless promotional abilities to his flourishing nursery business when, quite by accident, he became involved in politics. The Surrey municipal council's decision to convert a local park into a gravel pit triggered a small community protest, and a group of neighbours persuaded Vander Zalm to become involved—he was, after all, knowledgeable about parks and plants, and Art Knapp's had donated some shrubs to the threatened park. Vander Zalm's pitch to the municipal council fell on deaf ears, but the incident did spark his interest in politics: "It got me mad enough that I said, 'I'll fix these guys. I'll run for council.' "

His first attempt to win a seat on Surrey municipal council, in December 1964, was unsuccessful, but the following year he was elected for the first of two two-year terms and became a popular figure in one of Canada's fastest-growing and largest municipalities. "I found as alderman that I really couldn't do all the things that I wanted to see done," he remembered. This frustration, combined with a genuine liking for the business of politics, encouraged him to take on the incumbent mayor, and in December of 1969 Vander Zalm was elected to serve for the first of three consecutive, highly controversial terms as mayor of Surrey.

Vander Zalm took an activist approach to local government leadership. He established numerous committees and commissions and became embroiled in arguments with W. A. C. Bennett's administration over municipal funding and social welfare policies. He never shied from taking on any senior level of government and was forever making headline-grabbing pronouncements on such subjects as drug abuse, pornography and nuclear power. One critic suggested that Surrey was the only municipality in the world with a foreign policy.

Throughout this period Vander Zalm remained active in his business, though he also began to consider larger political challenges. His parents, like many immigrants to Canada, had supported the federal government of the day, and primarily through his father's influence, Vander Zalm was a strong Liberal. Never too concerned with ideology, he believed in Liberalism because of its apparent moderation. In fact, he viewed himself as a moderate, though increasingly he was aware that others saw him in a different light. He said later:

> If I was to peg myself on a scale of what's left or what's right, I would have to put myself in the middle—although that's not where people tend to put me, because what comes out when I'm on the hustings are my pronouncements on various moral issues or work ethic issues. And on those I come out fairly right-wing. When it's social issues, though, I tend to be a moderate. I have found myself to be in those positions for most of the time I've been involved in politics.

Before becoming mayor of Surrey, Vander Zalm had run as a Liberal candidate in the 1968 federal election, losing to the NDP candidate. He was one of only a handful of unsuccessful B.C. Grits not carried along to Ottawa in the exciting wave of Trudeaumania —indeed, British Columbia was second only to Quebec in embracing the country's new, charismatic Liberal leader. Vander Zalm's other experience with Liberalism occurred in 1972 when the leader of the provincial party, Dr. Pat McGeer, stepped down, causing a leadership convention. The mayor of Surrey, increasingly at odds with Victoria, decided to throw his hat into the ring even though the party's five MLAs, including the outgoing leader, unanimously endorsed a young Liberal MP, David Anderson. Vander Zalm criticized "the appearance of old-time politics" and looked forward to the convention, saying: "If I can't convince them on the convention floor, I'd just as soon not have it." The urbane Grits were not about to elect as their leader a radical, immigrant, local politician whose keynote address at the convention was an appeal to "whiplash drug pushers, cut off welfare deadbeats, update education, crack down on wife-deserters and provide government-financed dental care." He lost to Anderson on the first ballot, 388 to 177.

Losses became as important as victories in Vander Zalm's budding political career. While Anderson's win led him nowhere, Vander Zalm had acquired the invaluable experience of fighting a provincial leadership contest. He also met many politicians who would play roles in his future, including Pat McGeer, Garde Gardom, Jack Davis and Mel Couvelier. And he began to question whether he belonged in the Liberal Party.

During his years as mayor of Surrey, Vander Zalm established his own enduring, sometimes endearing, often perplexing political style. Politics for him was a series of challenges, the pursuit of which motivated all of his energies and considerable charm. But once these challenges were met, he felt empty until new goals could be set. Every two years, when it came time to decide whether or not to seek re-election, he would wait until the last moment before making his decision. To be fair, he had family and business responsibilities to consider, but he also delighted in the attention brought on by uncertainty. And he wanted people to coax him to run again.

Vander Zalm's style of leadership often blurred the normal distinctions of business, family and politics. He and his wife were strong community people, and they often invited groups such as pensioners to their home for strawberry teas, or else quietly helped out cases of hardship. Rita Johnston, an alderman on Vander Zalm's council, said:

> I can remember going into his office and he would say: "Rita, we've got these people with a problem. And Lillian's trying to gather up some sheets and pillowcases because they're poor and they need as much help as they can get. Do you know anybody that has some, or do you have any spare ones at home?" Now, that's not normally what you'd expect the mayor to be doing. When he'd hear of a hardship case he'd be right in there.

From his bailiwick in suburban Surrey, Vander Zalm had been an outspoken critic of the province's Social Credit government, and in 1972, when the NDP defeated W. A. C. Bennett's government, the stage was set for another try at provincial politics. Bill Bennett, the new Socred leader, rallied the forces of private enterprise against the socialist regime of Dave Barrett. Bennett's recruitment program for new Social Credit members and potential candidates for the next election attracted adherents of other political faiths, and on 29 May 1974 Bill Vander Zalm became the first of several prominent provincial Liberals to join Bill Bennett's team. He obtained a Socred nomination in his home riding of Surrey and in December of 1975 was elected to the new provincial government.

Right from the start Premier Bennett recognized that Bill Vander Zalm was a popular politician with a strong base of support, and appointed him to the sensitive cabinet post of Human Resources. Vander Zalm immediately set a new tone for this ministry—and for the government—by making his famous statement about employable welfare recipients: "If anybody is able to work, but refuses to pick up the shovel, we will find ways of dealing with him." Vander Zalm quickly turned this potentially damaging statement to positive effect. At Socred party functions he auctioned off gold-painted shovels; he also sold hundreds of sterling silver lapel shovels with membership cards in the Loyal Order of Shovellers, raising over $85,000 for the party. Thus he made the shovel his political trademark, a symbol of hard work, contact with the earth and free enterprise. The grassroots of the Social Credit Party began a lasting love affair with the dashing new politician who signed his personal notes "Happy Shovelling."

Vander Zalm continued to attract province-wide attention as, unlike most other ministers, he travelled extensively throughout British Columbia, energetically defending the government's policies and always willing to listen to the concerns of party members. At Social Credit Party functions, the applause was often as loud for Vander Zalm as it was for Premier Bennett. His enthusiasm, accessibility and popularity lent some credence to press rumours of leadership aspirations. To such suggestions Vander Zalm responded: "I'm a great guy for challenges, so when Bill Bennett steps down I'll probably be in there pitching with the best of them." But there was no real evidence that Vander Zalm was a rival for the Socred leadership. He demonstrated the utmost respect for Bill Bennett, always referring to him as "the premier" or "Mr. Premier," and none of Vander Zalm's office staff, ministry officials or cabinet colleagues can recall any overt signs that he was out to usurp his boss.

Nevertheless, Bennett felt he had good reason to keep Vander Zalm in the unpopular Human Resources portfolio. Not only was it a large, complex ministry with a huge budget but it was characterized by the grinding difficulty of dealing with hardship cases day after day. It was also a highly political job, for the NDP, criticized as a spendthrift government, had allowed $100-million spending overruns in Human Resources, and it was Vander Zalm's mandate to regain control of expenditures. He cracked down hard on assumed widespread welfare fraud, centralized administrative control of most social services and scrapped the Vancouver Resources Board which, for him, was an unnecessary level of bureaucracy with little accountability.

On his own terms, Bill Vander Zalm succeeded in meeting his goals; in his first year he showed more than a $100-million budget surplus for his ministry. As a result, a strong cry of protest rose up from those who believed that he was holding back welfare payments from the needy, and the opposition branded him as cruel and mean-spirited. A political cartoon by Bob Bierman, published in the Victoria *Times* in 1978, showed Vander Zalm gleefully picking the wings off flies. Vander Zalm, in what became a landmark case for freedom of the press, launched a libel action in the

Supreme Court of B.C.; he won his case and was awarded damages, though the B.C. Court of Appeal subsequently overturned the ruling.

Vander Zalm's reputation for controversy easily extended beyond British Columbia's borders. To Canadians east of the Rockies, he was the archetypal west coast politician, frequently making headlines with outrageous and colourful remarks. When the Parti Québécois was elected in 1976, he said he would not lose any sleep over the prospect of Quebec leaving confederation—at least he would no longer have to put up with bilingual Corn Flakes boxes. Vander Zalm was delighted with the publicity that such comments never failed to stir up; for months afterward he was asked to autograph Corn Flakes boxes.

In 1979 Vander Zalm again made national headlines on a Quebec issue. At a Socred Party meeting, he sang a song in which he referred to Premier René Lévesque as a frog. He was immediately branded as a bigot and a racist. The national media accused him of trying to wreck confederation; civil rights activists called for his resignation; the Edmonton *Journal* published a cartoon which showed him pulling the legs off frogs. Such widespread attention only encouraged Vander Zalm. "The things I say are probably what a lot of people are thinking," he said. "Other politicians would like to talk that way, but they wouldn't dare because they think they'll get a lot of heat and flak."

In Premier Bennett's pre-election cabinet shuffle in late 1978, Vander Zalm was moved to the portfolio of Municipal Affairs, while Grace McCarthy was given the difficult Human Resources post. Vander Zalm, re-elected in the 1979 general election, tackled his new cabinet responsibilities with considerable enthusiasm. Although as a minister of the crown he rarely became involved in the administration of his ministry, he was very active in matters of policy. Because the public service in British Columbia was weak in expertise and experience, an activist minister such as Vander Zalm was afforded plenty of opportunity to develop and implement policy—a contrast to the position of ministers elsewhere who are too often the figureheads for powerful, entrenched bureaucracies.

Bill Vander Zalm's education in government and public policy has come largely from bureaucrats. He respected the advice of his civil servants and developed strong and enduring relationships with those who worked with him closely. In his ministries, he knew officials down to executive director level by their first names. And he filled senior ministry vacancies from within, rather than recruit from outside. The most common complaint of his civil servants was that they were never certain of ministry policy until they had read the morning newspaper.

As minister of municipal affairs, Vander Zalm pressed forward with an urban transit system for Vancouver and the Lower Mainland, ignoring recommendations for further studies or consultation. His decision would result in expenditures of more than $1 billion and the realization of SkyTrain, North America's most advanced light rapid transit system. He also launched the controversial land use bill to reorganize and centralize planning and administration of local government in British Columbia. Vander Zalm stubbornly promoted his bill for three years before the cabinet pulled the plug on it in the dying moments of the 1982 legislative session. The frustrated minister came close to resigning, and he publicly criticized the cabinet's inaction as "gutless."

Vander Zalm's falling out with the cabinet and his increasing restlessness coincided with the rise of Premier Bennett's new, professionalized office and "tough guy" image. As a cabinet minister, Vander Zalm was never considered an outsider, because Bill Bennett's stoical style did not allow for insiders—there was never any evidence of an inner cabinet during Bennett's premiership. But clearly his new style alienated some cabinet ministers more than others, and Vander Zalm found himself increasingly at odds with the premier's office. He never criticized the premier directly; nor was Bennett ever openly critical of Vander Zalm, though he later described him as "very self-sufficient" as a minister.

Bennett shuffled his cabinet in the summer of 1982, signalling an election on the horizon. It was thought Vander Zalm might be shuffled right out of the cabinet, but instead he was reappointed. The minister's policy adviser, Derek De Biasio, recalled:

He came in and said: "Derek, Derek, guess what? The premier's given me a new cabinet position. Now, what do you think is the last cabinet position that I would get?"

I said: "Labour."

He said: "No, it's not Labour. What do you think is the second last?"

I said: "Education."

He said: "Yeah, Education!"

He was quite excited about it. But I remember at the time it was quite humorous. We were both laughing our heads off.

Vander Zalm, who later admitted that he was "not the most likely ministerial material for Education," believed he was given the assignment to help introduce the government's restraint program. "It was realized by the Spectors and the Kinsellas and whoever else was advising Bill Bennett that this was not going to be a popular program, and whoever took it on was going to get hammered pretty hard." So the post was both a form of punishment and a convenient appointment because Vander Zalm was so resilient to hammering.

Vander Zalm saw Bennett's deputy minister, Norman Spector, as the engineer of restraint and believed he seriously upset Spector's plans by not strictly following the script that was written for his new cabinet post.

I was told by Spector: "You've got to go on the restraint theme and don't you dare talk about other things."

And I said: "Well, hold it just a minute. I'm minister of education, and obviously I'm going to talk about things related to education as well as talk about restraint. I'm not here as minister responsible for restraint."

So I spoke out about things like the quality of education, and how we could provide a better curriculum for the youngsters, and how the basics—reading, writing, arithmetic, history—should be the priority as opposed to field trips and the like. And I even got into very controversial things like, should we recite the Lord's Prayer in the classroom? When I got involved in all these sorts of issues, that didn't follow the plan.

I can recall Norman Spector coming to me being quite critical of the fact that I was talking about these things. He said: "Stick with restraint. Your job is restraint." I didn't listen to Norman Spector of course, because he wasn't my boss.

In the nine months that Bill Vander Zalm served in the Education portfolio, he not only struggled with internal political pressures but also fought with new outside pressure groups such as the British Columbia Teachers Federation (BCTF). In addition to his strongly expressed views on curriculum and classroom activities, Vander Zalm made frequent provocative pronouncements on the need for better management in public schools and less political action on the part of the BCTF. In fact, he became so endeared to the BCTF that at one of their rallies they left behind for him a gift of dead flowers and extra-strength Tylenol capsules—at the time of the poisoned Tylenol scare in the United States.

Vander Zalm was concerned about the "stifling and bureaucratic" direction the Bennett government was heading in. As well, there were unsubtle suggestions that he was no longer wanted as a member of Bill Bennett's team and that he could not be guaranteed a cabinet position after the election. "It bothered me for a long time, and I'd been thinking about it more and more," he said. "I went to bed every night and my last thought was: 'What am I doing here? Should I carry on?' "

Unhappy with his lot in Victoria, frustrated by what he saw as lack of support from the premier's office, and realizing that he no longer enjoyed politics, Vander Zalm announced in April 1983 that he would not seek re-election and took what he called a sabbatical. According to Derek De Biasio, Vander Zalm does not think people should make a lifelong career of politics: "He thinks there should be change and revitalization. He thought it was a good time to get out. He was still young enough that he knew he could come back at a later time."

Some of his colleagues harshly criticized Vander Zalm for not contesting the tense and bitter 1983 election. Amidst predictions of a defeat for the government, Vander Zalm was seen as a rat deserting a sinking ship. Yet nothing suggests that he was in danger of defeat in his home riding. As well, had the government been defeated, Vander Zalm would have been well positioned to take a run at the party leadership. As it turned out, he would benefit from not being part of the post-1983 Socred team, whose tougher phase of restraint produced massive public protests.

There was one other reason why Bill Vander Zalm left provincial politics in 1983. The side of politics that most voters rarely see and that takes the greatest toll on a politician's life is the family that so often gets left behind. Vander Zalm was sensitive to the needs of his family but, at the same time, aware of the insensitivities bred by politics:

Once you're in politics and you take a liking to it and you know you can do it and you start to take on challenges that you want to see through, it's hard to let go. But it's a real sacrifice because your whole life becomes just that. There's very little time for family. If I could go back and do it all over again, I would like to take more time for family. Doing more things with the kids is the one thing I really missed out on.

That the Vander Zalms successfully withstood the pressures of politics undoubtedly owes much to the strength and enthusiasm of Lillian. A classic woman-behind-the-man, she is an important political asset to her husband, for in addition to their appearing together in public, she has become his closest and most influential confidante. In their thirty-year marriage they seem to share everything and are rarely apart for long. They never disagree in public and always know what is on each other's mind. Their religious faith has cemented their relationship with simple but powerful certitudes. They believe that the world is meant to be a good place and that among people there is a force towards good. This is not destiny, but a goal that must be worked for. According to Vander Zalm: "We don't get down about things if they don't go as we expected them to. You get your setbacks and you get your hurts, but you know that if you accept them and push on and do what you believe to be right, that it will turn out the way it's supposed to in the end."

Although Vander Zalm's orthodox religious convictions are sprinkled with a belief in ESP and numerology, his devout Catholicism goes unquestioned and has shaped most of his views on the social and moral issues of the day. While on his self-proclaimed sabbatical, he organized the visit to British Columbia of Pope John Paul II, an event he has described as one of the highlights of his life. A mass celebrated by the pontiff before a massive crowd at Abbotsford airport, followed by a similar event at a packed B.C. Place stadium, were juxtaposed against Operation Solidarity's antirestraint rallies. Vander Zalm overlooked those protests and said of the papal visit: "What's so beautiful about all this—and I hope it lasts when it's all over—is that we've had the opportunity to show that British Columbians can get together when the cause is there and pull together."

Other events during Vander Zalm's busy sabbatical ensured that he stayed in the public eye. He hosted a radio garden show, often entertaining listeners with political comments; he wrote a series of gardening columns for the Vancouver *Sun*, and he published a popular book, *The Northwest Gardener's Almanac*. His most ambitious venture was the purchase of a botanical garden in Richmond which he and his wife have transformed into a sprawling twenty-one-acre, multimillion-dollar theme park and tourist attraction called Fantasy Garden World. The Vander Zalms poured tremendous energy into this dream; within a year of purchasing the original site they were granted approval for at least fifteen expansions, including the construction of a conservatory, a bell tower, chapel, gazebo, barn, animal shelters, railway station, parking lot, restaurants and garden centre complex. In time they expanded further, even acquiring a Dutch castle.

The rapid growth of Fantasy Gardens was a contentious issue for some municipal politicians and town planners. Because part of the land to be developed was within the province's agricultural land reserve, Vander Zalm was forced to apply to the Agricultural Land Commission for its removal from the reserve. He also faced many hurdles with his bankers, but his persistence, even obstinacy, made Fantasy Gardens both a well-known attraction and a colourful home base.

By far the greatest challenge to the success of this venture was the lure of a return to politics, for Vander Zalm could never willingly rid himself of a craving for public recognition and power. Shortly after he left Victoria, Grace McCarthy, among others, urged him to consider a return to municipal politics by taking a run at the mayoralty of Vancouver in 1984. But Vander Zalm was too uncertain of his chances, and, besides, his mind was focussed on his new business. Yet the chance to serve as mayor of Vancouver during the city's centennial year and Expo 86 was difficult to completely dismiss.

For almost a year he played a will-he, won't-he game of speculation while the civic Non-Partisan Association (NPA) wooed him as their candidate to oust Mayor Mike Harcourt and his left-leaning city council. Finally, Vander Zalm decided against running and called a news conference at Fantasy Gardens.

At a breakfast meeting on the day of his announcement, an NPA delegation tried one last time to persuade Vander Zalm that without someone of his stature running, Harcourt would win re-election by acclamation. Vander Zalm began to waver. Ten minutes before the news conference, his friend John Plul of radio station CKNW arrived to offer support for what he believed would be Vander Zalm's announcement that he was running. Vander Zalm pulled Plul aside and asked him a few urgent questions about the NPA's organization and their campaigning ability. With Plul's confident replies in mind, Vander Zalm moments later discarded his prepared news releases and declared his candidacy for the mayoralty of Vancouver.

It was an unusual start to an equally unusual contest. Unfortunately for Vander Zalm, his last-minute decision meant a poorly organized campaign. As well, Mayor Harcourt effectively portrayed him as an interloper, a suburban politician who had walked across the Fraser River in his wooden shoes to assume the civic leadership of a city he had never lived in. The politics of personality that now manifested itself had a bitter, uncivil tone. Aside from describing his opponent as a "foreign import" and refusing to call him by name, Harcourt further infuriated Vander Zalm with his characteristically moderate, almost ambiguous policy stances.

That Harcourt, a former NDP provincial candidate, was running against a former Socred cabinet minister inevitably introduced to the election a heightened sense of partisanship, which, with the backdrop of the unpopular Social Credit restraint program, did little to help Vander Zalm's campaign. The Social Credit Party organization itself offered him little in the way of support.

With only a couple of weeks to go, Vander Zalm's campaign lagged badly, and his NPA handlers urged him to make a tougher, more ideological attack on his opponents to bring out the vote on the affluent west side of the city. He launched into an aggressive, paranoid style of campaign, even accusing "the ultra-left Harcourt-COPE coalition" (COPE stands for Committee of Progressive Electors) of having ties to the Soviet Union. Vander Zalm realized too late that this tactic was a mistake.

On election day—17 November—he was trounced by Harcourt, who received 62 per cent of the vote. There was no question that Vander Zalm had province-wide appeal and could pack community halls throughout rural, small-town British Columbia, but in Vancouver his charm and his issues were lost on an urban audience who could easily accept Mike Harcourt's ambiguity over so potent a mixture of populism and paranoia. There was no love lost between the re-elected mayor and his challenger, who ignored the usual courtesy of conceding defeat and offering congratulations on election night.

No doubt the defeat was an important political lesson. It also denied Vander Zalm the opportunity to be mayor of Vancouver during the exciting Expo 86 celebrations. But it also left him available for the Socred leadership when Bill Bennett stepped down. "I believe that somehow destiny has its role," Vander Zalm mused.

The defeat had a somewhat mellowing effect on Vander Zalm, and, aside from activities in service clubs and the chamber of commerce, he now devoted most of his energies to his fledgling business at Fantasy Garden World. His political career up to this point was a catalogue of victories and defeats, and he always believed there would be another day, another contest. But for a supposedly ambitious politician, his style lacked intensity and focus. Certainly he was not clawing his way to power, and he was fatalistic in defeat. Many wondered if his political career was finally over after the 1984 Vancouver election, but when Bill Bennett announced his retirement in May of 1986 a more cautious, more mature Bill Vander Zalm was forced to wrestle once again with ambition. His friend and business adviser Peter Toigo remembered Vander Zalm saying: "If this was five years ago, it would be 80 per cent ego and 20 per cent that I could do a good job. But today, where I am in life, it's 20 per cent ego and 80 per cent that I know I can really do a good job for this province."

When he entered the race to succeed Bennett as leader and as premier he was not sure he could win—he was in fact less confident of victory than in almost any previous political contest. However, he felt compelled to run, and his last-minute decision to seek the leadership was based on intuition and a belief that no matter what the outcome, he could not lose. He was both unafraid of failure and certain that his candidacy would produce widespread, free publicity for his Fantasy Gardens.

In politics, one discovers how far it is possible to go only by travelling in a straight line until one is stopped. At Whistler, on 30 July 1986, Bill Vander Zalm could not be stopped. His dramatic victory was never assured, but on balloting day the delegates exercised their free will in an unencumbered fashion, allowing the outsider to triumph. The establishment candidates, arguing amongst themselves, were unable to organize a Stop Vander Zalm movement, and the convention was clearly in the hands of the party's grassroots, not the political machines. Vaughn Palmer of the Vancouver *Sun* wrote: "If you'd wanted a system that would give the edge to a poorly organized, poorly funded, but highly charismatic populist, you couldn't have come up with a better one." Columnist Marjorie Nichols summed up Vander Zalm's victory: "The neo-conservative Social Credit machine built by Bill Bennett is dead, the victim of a freakish head-on collision with a grassroots bulldozer driven by an unelected rampaging populist." Jack Davis, the maverick MLA who had supported the winner from the time he announced his candidacy, said on the convention floor: "The grassroots has been victorious over Patrick Kinsella." And Bill Vander Zalm declared it "the triumph of the shovel over the machine."

Although there were moments of uneasiness during that tense day of voting, Vander Zalm concluded that his victory was meant to be:

> The Bud Smith crossover was perhaps one of the most exciting moments in the whole of that exercise. It was very exciting. It was good television. And it's what people tend to remember. I frankly don't think it made a great difference in the outcome. I'm grateful to Bud Smith in that I think it took some courage on his part because he had to go against his own advisers who were telling him to go to Brian Smith. But I don't believe that Couvelier and Reynolds and those people coming over, or even Bud Smith walking across the floor, made that great a difference. It would have gone that way anyhow.

Clearly Vander Zalm would not have been Bennett's personal choice as his successor. The outgoing premier was satisfied, though, that Vander Zalm was a popular choice who undoubtedly had the ability to win the next election and therefore maintain power for the party. Bennett was, however, concerned about the new leader's ability to face the complex challenge of managing a government. And he likely would have preferred a successor whose personality, temperament and leadership style were closer to his own.

In the wake of Vander Zalm's win, most Socreds forgot about the supposed conspiracy of succession that had so fiercely motivated some of the contenders. There was no sign now of the presumed head start, the set-up amongst party insiders, the alleged plan for an orderly transfer of leadership to a chosen successor. Grace McCarthy later said:

> We'll never be able to prove that there was a set-up. There's no proof, because it didn't happen. But I think it could have happened if people had been asleep, or if people didn't care, or if people were hoodwinked. But nobody was hoodwinked. And maybe in retrospect people want to change their minds. Maybe they find it more comfortable to look back on things as they would have liked them to be rather than as they really were. We all would like to do that. But the reality is, there were people who had a head start—a country-mile head start—on the leadership campaign. That was unquestionably there.

In politics, shared fears or hatreds are almost always the basis of friendships. Grace McCarthy wanted to win at Whistler, but she also wanted to prevent others from winning. Bill Vander Zalm's victory was therefore a happy outcome for the matriarch of the Social Credit Party:

> I was very relieved it turned out the way it did, because I felt it was in the right hands at the right time in the province's history. And that was important to me. I felt Bill Vander Zalm was a person who could be as populist a leader as was W. A. C. Bennett, whom I admired very much, and as strongly free enterprise as I was. And it was what Bill Bennett had ordered when he resigned—a new, fresh look. And he got what he wanted. So, in a way, everybody's needs were satisfied.

Although McCarthy lamented the end of the Bennett era, she welcomed the "new, fresh" approach. She believed the party had collectively made the right choice, and it was the choice that was going to keep the socialists out of office so the Socreds could help the province recover from the recession.

The morning after his triumph, Vander Zalm met with Premier Bennett, the first step in the transfer of power. Later that morning he met with Grace McCarthy to discuss the challenges ahead. McCarthy reminded the premier-elect of the time he had almost

resigned from the cabinet, and she remembered then quoting
W. A. C. Bennett: "Don't get mad. Get even." She said to Vander
Zalm: "Well, you certainly did get even, didn't you, Bill?"

More than thirteen years earlier, when Bill Bennett had won the
Social Credit leadership, he went out of his way to emphasize: "I
am my own man." Now his successor told the news media: "I'm a
new man." Vander Zalm was reacting to the apprehension greeting
his election, which was based upon vivid memories of him as a
shoot-from-the-lip cabinet minister who made confrontation his
hallmark, and as a commie-bashing mayoral candidate in Vancouver. "I can be nonconfrontational," he said, "and I will be."

Bill Vander Zalm continued to distance himself from his predecessor. His leadership campaign had stressed the differences
between himself and Bill Bennett and, in that sense at least, his
victory can be seen as a repudiation of the pre-Whistler party
leadership. The Socreds, like the public, were tired of restraint
and the Bennett government's tough-minded public policy.
Vander Zalm capitalized on this mood by presenting himself as an
anti-Bennett candidate who would end the era of confrontation
and fear and bring the Good Life back to British Columbia. His
first several months in office were spent reinforcing this essential
difference, to the chagrin of some party members and Bennett
loyalists, who felt he carried the theme too far.

For Social Credit in British Columbia the ability to hand the
torch of leadership from one party leader to another seems to require some cataclysmic event. The government's defeat in 1972
impelled the party to rebuild, allowing it to recapture the reins of
power in 1975, even though most observers had written the party
off. Then in 1986, when Bill Bennett announced his retirement,
many predicted that this time Social Credit was surely headed the
way of the dinosaurs. But no one could have foreseen the rise of
Bill Vander Zalm. The motto of this populist protest party seems
to be Revolution, Not Evolution. Certainly Social Crediters in
British Columbia are uninterested in the orderly kind of succession
assumed of political elites by political scientists. Rather, they are
drawn to an unorthodox form of internal regeneration. Once the
outsiders become insiders, once the disenfranchised become the
establishment, it is time for a thorough house cleaning.

Vander Zalm's win promised the kind of sweeping renewal more
commonly associated with a wholesale change of government than

with a mere switch of party leaders. His leadership campaign had been based upon a complete rejection of the party establishment, the party organization and the party fund raisers. Within days of becoming premier he launched an investigation into connections between the Sentinel Group, the consulting firm run by Mike Burns and Patrick Kinsella, and the previous administration— more the act of an opposition leader who had come to power than of a member of the same political family. Certainly the Sentinel Group would have no influence in Bill Vander Zalm's Victoria. Never before had the new leader of a major Canadian party so completely turned his back on the well-developed party apparatus. In this sense, Vander Zalm's victory represents the triumph of populism, personality and the politics of protest.

Norman Spector, before he left Ottawa to serve as the Mulroney government's senior constitutional adviser, prepared detailed transition briefings similar to those he had given Bill Bennett after the 1983 general election. It was left to Jerry Lampert, as principal secretary in the premier's office, to deliver these documents to Vander Zalm and to advise him on transition issues. When Lampert asked Vander Zalm whom among his advisers he could liaise with on the issues of the moment, he was pointed to Bill Goldie of the B.C. Chamber of Commerce, a key Vander Zalm organizer at the leadership convention who, as it turned out, would have little ongoing connection with the premier. Lampert, who stayed for only a short time as principal secretary, was surprised at the absence of either an organized transition team or individuals appointed to deal with specific policy areas. He later said it is likely that the briefing books were never opened.

A week after Whistler, on 6 August 1986, Bill Vander Zalm was sworn in as the twenty-seventh premier of British Columbia. He was the province's third Social Credit premier and the first non-Bennett Socred premier. At the swearing-in ceremony he spoke of introducing "a spirit of co-operation" and talked about consultation and discussion as the best ways to resolve differences. However, he also gave his commitment to work for *all* British Columbians, "not for special interest groups or those with the shrillest voice." And he promised to do "not what is expedient, but what is right." He spoke of ethics and integrity and indicated that he planned to review conflict of interest regulations for those who held public office—an obvious swipe at the previous administration, which had been plagued by scandals and questionable behaviour on the part of several cabinet ministers. "Mistakes will be made, there will be errors," said Premier Vander Zalm, "but I tell you now they will be honest errors."

On his first official day as premier he also emphasized the virtues of family life. At the swearing-in ceremony, where he was flanked by his wife and children, he said that "the foundation of any successful society is the family unit." Afterward the Vander Zalms, their sons and daughters, spouses and friends showed up at the parliament buildings to try the premier's office on for size. It was a demonstration of a family pride not seen before in the oppressively formal environs of the legislative precinct, and it was in stark contrast to the serious and staid business atmosphere that had permeated the premier's office during Bill Bennett's years. A closed, working premiership was giving way to an open, social premiership with a visible first family at the helm.

The weekend after he became premier, Bill Vander Zalm travelled to Edmonton for his first test on the national stage, the annual first ministers' conference. Many commentators watched closely for a slip of tongue from the premier, an outrageous quote or a colourful statement. But then and in the weeks following, the accessible but cautious rookie premier who impressed almost everyone with his conciliatory, almost statesmanlike demeanour disappointed those political observers and opposition critics who were waiting for a glimpse of the old, controversial Bill Vander Zalm.

Because Vander Zalm's ascension to the premiership did not coincide with a general election, he was compelled to select his cabinet from among the ranks of the Social Credit caucus, which did not give him much room to manoeuvre in putting a fresh face on his administration. Then several veterans resigned—cabinet ministers Jack Heinrich, Bob McClelland, Tom Waterland and Bill Ritchie—giving the premier an opportunity to put his own stamp on the government.

The appointment of the new nineteen-member executive council represented the first stage of the official changing of the guard in Victoria. Vander Zalm surprised many by assuming responsibility for the finance portfolio. This was both a throwback to W. A. C. Bennett's years and a shrewd political move for an outsider returning to Victoria and wanting to quickly reacquaint himself with gov-

ernment administration. Grace McCarthy received the post of economic development (precisely what she requested) and, significantly, she was also given back the title of deputy premier, which
Bill Bennett had stripped her of following the 1983 general elec-
tion. Brian Smith, whose name had been on the final ballot at
Whistler, retained his position as attorney general, and others who
were kept on in their former offices included Pat McGeer, Garde
Gardom, Russ Fraser, Alex Fraser and Terry Segarty. Hugh
Curtis, who lost finance, was moved to the position of provincial
secretary, while Tony Brummet was switched to education and
Jim Hewitt had fisheries added to his agriculture portfolio. Claude
Richmond became the new minister of social services and housing;
Environment Minister Austin Pelton also took on responsibility for
parks; and Jack Kempf, the independent northerner, only recently
elevated to cabinet, became the province's powerful minister of
forests and lands. Elwood Veitch served in consumer and corporate
affairs, while leadership candidate Jim Nielsen was minister of
health.

He also brought into cabinet the three backbench MLAs who had
staunchly supported his leadership bid—Jack Davis, Rita Johnston
and Bill Reid—thus signalling that personal loyalties would be crucial during his premiership.

Vander Zalm was pleased to have two women—Grace McCarthy
and Rita Johnston—in his cabinet because of the "intuitive
talents" that he said women could bring to decision making: "Very
often women have extrasensory perception. Women have much
more of this than men. Women also have lots more intuition than
men." Under normal circumstances, Vander Zalm's ESP comments
would have been the brunt of severe and widespread criticism.
However, the premier was being embraced by a positive public
which seemed to willingly suspend such criticism. It is not surprising that a public weary of confrontation and bludgeoned for so
many years by the tough-minded Bennett administration believed
in the promise of renewal and welcomed the new government with
optimism. Vander Zalm reinforced this mood by quickly settling a
contract dispute with the 34,000-member B.C. Government Employees Union, offering them a no-concession salary increase, thus
signalling a possible end to public sector restraint. And as a gesture
towards his goal of "downsizing" government, he eliminated the

Ministry of Lands, Parks and Housing and divided its parts among three other ministries.

Bill Bennett and his powerful office had been smoothly replaced by an energetic, freewheeling leader engaged in a love affair with the news media and the public. Cabinet ministers, especially the holdovers from the previous administration, felt invigorated. "There was a feeling of greater independence because the office had gone," recalled Garde Gardom. The cabinet was supportive from the beginning because, Vander Zalm said, "I assured them that they were going to be part of the process, they were going to be involved, they were going to be consulted." Vander Zalm told his ministers that they were not going to be "bullied about by a deputy from the premier's office. That was one big leftover fear that I faced the day I walked in."

Of course there were more serious wounds to heal within the Social Credit Party following Whistler. There were the inevitable tensions and hurt feelings which result from hard-fought leadership races. There were questions about whether the unelected candidates would ultimately play a role in the new government. Interestingly, this postconvention infighting did not take place between the camps of the winner and his opponents, but rather amongst the losers. Vander Zalm remained unmoved and untouched by all the struggles for influence and position among supporters of Grace McCarthy, Brian Smith, Bud Smith and other leadership contenders.

Shortly after he became premier, Vander Zalm described his job as "a piece of cake." He said the only surprise was that it had been so easy to assume the office, finding his move into the premier's office less difficult than his earlier moves into cabinet portfolios: "I no longer felt the frustrations of having to do things in a particular way that was contrary to my personal gut feel. Instead of being a loyal sergeant following orders, suddenly I was a general calling the shots."

Vander Zalm's few appointments to high-profile positions frustrated some of those who had supported his leadership campaign and now expected their due rewards. The premier asked Jerry Lampert to remain as principal secretary for a short time to help out with the transition and the preparations for an election campaign. He also called an old friend, Bill Long, who had served as his deputy minister in municipal affairs, to assist with some of the most pressing public issues of the day. On Jerry Lampert's recommendation, Vander Zalm appointed David Poole to the position of executive director of the Social Credit Party. Poole was executive assistant to cabinet minister Elwood Veitch and had worked on Grace McCarthy's leadership campaign. Vander Zalm instructed him to prepare for either a series of by-elections or a general election.

The premier had recognized that sooner or later he would have to go to the people. The political climate now was right, with a rejuvenated party, wide public approval of the change in government leadership and a summer of celebration focussed on Expo 86. As an unelected premier, Vander Zalm would either have to run in one of the pending by-elections caused by the resignations in government ranks or call a general election. Although his advisers were almost unanimous that he should proceed with a provincial election, the premier was enjoying his political honeymoon and preferred to establish a bit of a track record in office before dropping an election writ. He also needed to familiarize himself with the pressing issues his government faced—and there were many.

Foremost was a labour dispute affecting the forest industry, a mainstay of the province's economy. The International Woodworkers of America (IWA) had been on strike almost from the time that Vander Zalm came to office, shutting down the sawmill operations of most of British Columbia's large, integrated forest products companies. It was not a typical labour contract battle over money but was, in union leader Jack Munro's view, a death-defying fight for job security and, in particular, protection of union members' jobs from further contracting out. For the forest companies, which had been severely ravaged by the recession and the restructuring world economy, this was a struggle for competitiveness and survival. Vander Zalm perceived the importance of the dispute and knew it could not be resolved as easily as the BCGEU contract settlement. He closely monitored the on-again, off-again negotiations and would have to weigh this strike in any election call.

Another issue affecting the industry was the American petition for a countervailing duty against Canadian lumber entering the United States. Most of the Canadian wood products exported to the U.S. were produced in British Columbia, and therefore a sizable duty would harm the provincial economy, jeopardizing some of British Columbia's less competitive mills and the jobs that went with them. This surge in American protectionism was a serious issue for the Vander Zalm administration, as it threatened to dampen prospects for British Columbia's economic recovery. It was also a complex matter, involving questions of whether Canadian industry and governments should be content to fight the threat of a duty through U.S. legal processes, or whether a negotiated settlement with the Americans was in order. Vander Zalm kept a close eye on the countervailing duty issue, for developments could influence the timing of an election.

One casualty of the recession was the twenty-year-old Bank of British Columbia, a key concern during the early period of Vander Zalm's premiership. The bank had been a raging behind-the-scenes political issue from about the time Edgar Kaiser Jr. had assumed its helm in 1984. Bill Bennett's finance minister, Hugh Curtis, later said that from early 1985 until August 1986, when he was removed from the portfolio by Vander Zalm, he "spent more time on the Bank of B.C. than any other single issue." It was a troublesome time for western Canadian banks; both the Northland and the Canadian Commercial banks had already failed, raising serious questions about the viability of regionally based financial institutions.

An aggressive activist, Kaiser had tried valiantly to save the Bank of B.C. and had initially done a remarkable job of restructuring the bank's liabilities. But his efforts were misunderstood and he himself was mistrusted. "Edgar had a reputation for being a little bit slippery, so we were always cautious about how we dealt with him," said Deputy Minister of Finance David Emerson. "He'd come over to Victoria and make very good presentations and try and railroad you and try to rush you into making a deal of some kind, to put equity in or do this or that."

In addition to encouraging the provincial government to support the bank, Kaiser worked on a variety of possible mergers with other financial institutions. On a dramatic weekend in the fall of 1985, Bennett's government believed the Bank of B.C. was about to complete a merger with one of Canada's "big five" banks, the Bank of Nova Scotia. The ministry of finance withdrew all of its deposits, totalling hundreds of millions of dollars, so that the Bank of Canada would provide replacement funding for the merger. Victoria thereby highlighted the question of whether provincial governments or the Bank of Canada should provide liquidity for Canada's banking system. As it turned out, the merger did not go through, and the following week the province returned its deposits to the Bank of B.C. However, the incident provoked a stormy exchange between Kaiser and the provincial government, with the bank chairman arguing that the withdrawal of government funds could have placed the bank in receivership.

Kaiser's energetic manoeuvring had been frustrated by Bennett's refusal of direct involvement and Curtis's refusal to communicate. Now Kaiser hoped that the new government would take a fresh approach and help to ensure the bank's survival, despite the possible hindrance of the rumours about his role at Whistler.

Unfortunately, the dream of maintaining an autonomous, regionally based bank died when the Bank of B.C. was sold late in 1986 to the Hongkong Bank of Canada. For Kaiser the sale represented a net loss to British Columbia, and he argued that the demise of the bank was not inevitable. He strongly believed that the provincial government could have taken a less passive stance and helped the bank through a critical period. "The cost would have been relatively minimal in terms of dollars, and the return enormous. What better leverage for the provincial dollar?" And even though Vander Zalm was the minister of finance, Kaiser faced the same frustrations that he had with Bennett. "You couldn't get Vander Zalm's time," he said. "You couldn't get his attention."

The premier's attention was generally focussed on the "Vander Zalm mania" sweeping the province. As if full-tilt on an election campaign, he and his wife travelled to small towns throughout British Columbia, testing the mood of the public, rarely mentioning government policy, just smiling, shaking hands and talking about a new day for B.C. Vander Zalm's broad grin seemed to lift the gloom from the province, and the politics of personality quickly elevated him to folk-hero status. Wherever he appeared, from small-town gatherings to the world's fair in Vancouver, he was greeted with an overwhelmingly positive response. And with his own good spirits and humour, he nurtured this mood. At the opening of the small Grantham Bridge in North Vancouver, he quipped: "My predecessor got to announce all the megaprojects, and I get the Grantham Bridge."

All of this had a salutary effect on the Social Credit Party. The leadership convention had attracted enough positive attention that more than ten thousand members had joined the party, and in the three months following Vander Zalm's victory another thirty thousand signed up. And now the party witnessed the start of fierce jockeying for nominations for the expected election.

The premier kept everyone guessing about the timing of the election. The opposition party in particular was thrown into disarray. Prior to Premier Bennett's retirement, the NDP had built an elaborate campaign strategy based upon a personal attack on Bill Bennett. Now they had to start anew. The prospect of an election campaign fought between the tough, serious Bill Bennett and the shy, bookish Bob Skelly had suggested an end to the politics of personality in British Columbia: a torpid contest of substance versus substance, with no style and no populism. However, the succession of Social Credit leadership and the rise of Bill Vander Zalm changed all that; the opposition was powerless to combat the charm and charisma of the new Socred leader.

Around this time Lisa Fitterman, an intrepid Vancouver *Sun* reporter, walked in on—and taped—a private chat between Bob Skelly and NDP MLA Emery Barnes, during which Skelly admitted: "I don't think we can campaign against Vander Zalm and the media coverage. That's just not something we can deal with." When Fitterman's story appeared under the front-page headline "NDP Fears Chances in Snap Poll," it was widely regarded as Bob Skelly's concession speech. But the election had not yet been announced.

Deftly juggling four key considerations, Premier Vander Zalm had decided that he needed a strong mandate to govern, and so a general election was unavoidable. The first consideration was the IWA strike, a dispute that would have precluded an election call under normal circumstances. Vander Zalm said:

> I had to gamble as to how long it would last. I thought that if during the course of the election period I could bring about a resolution, I'd win by it. If a resolution came about naturally, because we didn't interfere, I'd win by it. But if the legislature had to be called back to legislate a solution, I'd win by it after a mandate, but I'd lose by it before a mandate. That was the number one consideration.

The second consideration was the Saskatchewan election which
had been called for 20 October by the Conservative government of
Grant Devine. According to Vander Zalm:

> I had to decide how much time I wanted to have between the Sas-
> katchewan election and my own election. I could see if I allowed too
> much time, I'd be caught with a situation where if the NDP in Sas-
> katchewan won, they would be so buoyed up, they'd move their to-
> tal army out to B.C. to work for Skelly. And if they lost, they would
> want to prove that they could win and still move out to B.C. So I
> had to follow very quickly on the heels of Grant Devine to avoid the
> shift of all the NDP organizers in Saskatchewan to B.C.

The third and fourth considerations were less gambles and more
calculated reasons to drop the writ sooner rather than later. The
premier—finance minister had debated waiting until spring 1987
before going to the people with a new budget and legislative program, but the government's financial forecasts steered him away
from this option:

> It became patently clear that a favourable sort of election budget
> was out of the question. I could not present the people with a whole
> lot of new program promises because the money simply wouldn't be
> there. Revenues were down. And expenditures were on the rise be-
> cause we had settled with the BCGEU—and we were faced with hav-
> ing to settle with the nurses and the health workers. So I couldn't
> see myself presenting that thrilling of a budget to the populace of
> British Columbia.
>   The fourth reason was that I knew we would have to, in the pro-
> cess of developing a program for economic recovery in British
> Columbia, present to the House a fairly controversial legislative
> package. It wouldn't be the sort of package we saw six, eight, ten
> years ago, where we introduced Pharmacare and other programs
> geared towards providing additional help to people.
>   So there was really no choice. I had to go when I did.

In fact, he probably would have gone sooner if it had been possible. But faced with no campaign organization in place and in-
sufficient time to nominate candidates, Social Credit executive
director David Poole, Jerry Lampert and others were holding him

back. But Vander Zalm's intuition was clearly telling him to go. On 24 September he ended weeks of suspense by announcing a general election for 22 October; he would be taking advantage of the opportunity bequeathed to him by his predecessor, for the twenty-eight-day election campaign would end nine days after the close of Expo 86, catching voters in an optimistic, proud mood.

The last provincial election had seen Social Credit win thirty-five seats and the NDP twenty-two. Now, at dissolution, the Socreds held thirty-two seats, the NDP twenty-one and the Conservatives one; three seats were vacant. Redistribution of the provincial electoral system now created an additional twelve seats for a total of sixty-nine MLAs in the House. For Vander Zalm this was another favourable legacy of the previous administration, for the majority of the new seats were in strong Social Credit ridings. Vander Zalm himself secured a nomination in the new dual-member Richmond riding, the home of Fantasy Garden World.

In kicking off the campaign, the premier made no formal policy statement, nor did he offer any detailed election planks or promises. He simply indicated that there was "a lot to be done" by his new government and "a mandate is certainly needed." Vander Zalm also boldly—and, as it turned out, correctly—predicted: "There's going to be sunshine for the next twenty-eight days."

Opposition leader Bob Skelly launched the NDP campaign in a decidedly different fashion. In a disastrous televised response to the premier's election announcement, Skelly tried to recite his party's policy proposals. Visibly nervous, he even tried to halt the broadcast, asking, "Can I stop this?" But this was not a dress rehearsal. The NDP had no excuse to be unprepared for the election announcement and yet their leader's nervousness only overshadowed his predictable policy proposals and election promises. It was the worst imaginable start to an election campaign. Skelly compounded his problems the following day when he explained his discomfort and stage fright with an embarrassing joke for which he later offered apologies to the premier. "I think I went out for lunch and ate the wrong kind of tulip bulbs," he said.

In dramatic contrast, Bill Vander Zalm was smiling, confident and self-assured. On his first full day of campaigning he fulfilled an earlier promise to visit a secluded Indian reserve at Kingcome Inlet. Meanwhile, the race was on for nominations, and the party's renewal continued. More long-time Socred warhorses announced their retirement from battle, including Hugh Curtis, Garde Gardom and Jim Nielsen. And among the successful nominations were leadership candidates Mel Couvelier, Bud Smith and Kim Campbell. Social Credit renewal also saw a huge wave of first-time candidates made up of small businessmen and municipal politicians, thus maintaining its populist base.

The NDP also quietly showed signs of renewal with a new generation of candidates trying hard to compensate for their party leader's inadequacies. Interestingly, almost half of the NDP nominees were tied to the education lobby—teachers, former teachers, or educational administrators—the group that had been so fiercely mobilized and poisoned by Bennett's restraint policies—and the other half were primarily either lawyers or came from the ranks of trade union leadership. The socialist party had clearly become a white-collar party. Amongst their candidates was one clear portent of change and renewal in the person of Vancouver mayor Mike Harcourt, running in the safe NDP riding of Vancouver-Centre.

The campaign saw a continuation of the polarization that had become such a dominant feature of British Columbia's two-party politics. Although several other parties did nominate candidates, only the Socreds and the NDP fielded full slates for the sixty-nine available seats. The provincial Liberals waged a lively and energetic effort under the leadership of Art Lee—they nominated fifty-five candidates. The provincial Tories were in disarray, fielding only twelve half-hearted standard-bearers. But as the campaign got underway the general expectation was of a landslide for the governing party under Vander Zalm's popular leadership. Indeed, the NDP were given less of a chance of winning than in any election in the past two decades. The 1986 contest was not to decide whether British Columbia would be governed by socialists or capitalists; it was a provincial referendum on the popularity of Bill Vander Zalm.

The NDP were in an unenviable position. The succession of Social Credit leadership, besides undermining their electoral strategy, had largely satisfied the province's hunger for change. The thirteen hundred Socred delegates at Whistler had already done the deed that the public was now being asked to endorse. Up against a seemingly insurmountable wall, the NDP could only experiment with tough attacks on Social Credit's new leader. Skelly, who demonstrated several more bouts of public nervousness, suggested that the new-image Vander Zalm had a secret agenda which he was afraid to reveal until after the election; he criticized the premier as all style and no substance and challenged him to debate the issues of the day; he also tried to tar Vander Zalm with the brush of Bennett's policies, saying, "I'm convinced that it was Vander Zalm who gave Bill Bennett the idea for restraint." Using a hard-edged, blunt advertising campaign which progressively chipped away at Vander Zalm's credibility, the NDP were forced to abandon their policy and were reduced to fighting the politics of personality.

The Socreds believed that such personal attacks could only backfire on the NDP. In private, the premier was in fact eager to accept the challenge of a televised debate with Skelly—"I can beat this guy," he told his campaign team. However, he reluctantly accepted the advice of campaign manager Poole and campaign chairman Lampert not to debate Skelly. Their reasoning was that the NDP had all the issues and all the policy proposals, while the Socreds had none. "Our campaign was thrown together, literally thrown together to capitalize on Bill Vander Zalm," said David Poole. "We had no policy. It was just Fresh Start—give this guy a chance. I believe the NDP didn't capitalize on it as they should have, partially because of the ineffectiveness of their leader."

The Socred campaign theme was summed up in their leader's slogan, Fresh Start. Vander Zalm emphasized new directions for government in British Columbia. And with the NDP virtually abandoning their planned assault on restraint, Vander Zalm picked up the theme, himself criticizing the implementation of restraint. He never argued with the goals of Bennett's program, but rather claimed that it had been executed in too harsh and confrontational a manner. He rarely, however, delved into substantive policy issues, believing that people voted for people, not issues. Vander Zalm remained uncommitted in his effort to win the hearts of the uncommitted.

For the first half of the campaign, Vander Zalm energetically charged around the province, usually accompanied by Lillian, an accomplished politician in her own right. The Vander Zalms were extending their romance with the people of British Columbia—an affair that began at Whistler. Wherever they appeared together, crowds mobbed them, posing for photographs, waiting for auto-

graphs and generally enjoying the upbeat feeling engendered by
the couple. And whether it was in small-town shopping malls or
main-streeting campaign hops, Vander Zalm played to them like a
political virtuoso. He greeted people openly and sincerely, truly
enjoying the politicking of politics. When talking with children,
senior citizens, concerned or aggrieved citizens, his heart was
always right up there in his face. The news media suspended their
skepticism and were content to let their cameras and tape recorders
document this political phenomenon. The telegenic premier's
best qualities invariably received wide play on province-wide television as he produced, directed and starred in his own twenty-
eight-day miniseries.

In many respects this election was dominated by a presidential-
style campaign, where all the attention focussed on the leader.
This created some nervousness for the sixty-eight other Socred
candidates. When the premier jaunted through their ridings on his
whirlwind tour, the local Socred candidates would stick closely to
him in the hope of receiving some media attention, voter recognition or at least a photograph taken with the star.

The campaign style also produced considerable anxiety for the
Social Credit election team, which seemed unable to exert much
control over the premier's itinerary. Vander Zalm gallivanted
around the province by bus and by plane, campaigning and simultaneously conducting government business by telephone, and he
was late for almost every campaign stop, for he often stayed too
long at events, mingling with the crowds. Only towards the end of
the campaign did he recognize that it was unacceptable to leave
people waiting two to three hours at each scheduled event. "He
thought he could run the campaign from the back of a pickup
truck," recalled David Poole, "that he and Lillian would travel
around saying 'Hi' to folks and he'd win." It fell to Poole to try to
impress upon Vander Zalm the need for control and organization.
This was a difficult challenge, but it was also the start of a growing
rapport between the two men.

Vander Zalm confused his election workers by criticizing his
own campaign as lavish and extravagant. He had sent out specific
orders that he wanted to spend less money than had been spent by
the party in the 1983 election, and he almost achieved this objective. He wanted a different kind of campaign than had been organized in the past and, aside from Jerry Lampert who remained in

the background, there was no evidence of input from the privy council of his predecessor. No doubt he got what he wanted, but this created difficulties for a new party leader with no experience of being in the eye of an election storm. Vander Zalm loved the attention and enjoyed the limelight but was increasingly forced to check his normally freewheeling style. His public musings now became government policy; this resulted in unusual public expectations, including legalized gambling, relaxed liquor regulations, an increased minimum wage and decreased beer prices. The most difficult challenge for Vander Zalm was pacing. His organizers marvelled at his stamina as, on the road day after day, he rose early each morning and slept only a few hours each night.

Midway through the campaign, the premier became involved in a daring labour relations mediation effort, attempting to single-handedly break the impasse in the IWA—forest industry dispute. He left Lillian to campaign on his behalf in the province's northwest and flew back to Vancouver to carry out the crucial negotiations. For more than twelve hours, first at an airport terminal and later at a hotel, Vander Zalm engaged in a tireless round of shuttle diplomacy, keeping the rivers of negotiation flowing, wanting desperately to succeed where labour relations professionals had failed. For the premier to be taking valuable time off from his campaign was a large gamble, but he believed an opportunity existed to break the stalemate in the lengthy dispute. Rather than delegate this task to his labour minister or to senior government officials, Vander Zalm took the responsibility upon himself, accompanied only by David Poole.

The talks broke off in failure beyond three o'clock the following morning. The two-month old strike continued, and the premier appointed a mediator. Vander Zalm was genuinely disappointed, but a settlement may have been impossible with a Social Credit leader intervening in negotiations with labour leader Jack Munro, a prominent NDP supporter. Vander Zalm commented to waiting reporters: "It's amazing how often you think you've almost got it, and then all of a sudden it slips away on you. Strange business, this. I don't want to do it again, or not too much of it anyway." He indicated that a legislated settlement might take place if the workers were not back on the job after the election. He also began to formulate plans which would prevent lengthy, crippling labour disputes in the future.

Premier Vander Zalm did not sleep at all that night, and within a few hours he was flying north to begin another full day of electioneering. He never visibly missed a beat, and if there was any slack in the next few days, Lillian picked it up for her exhausted mate. But the premier and his organizers remembered this period as a kind of watershed in the campaign. "That was about the time it slowed down," said Vander Zalm. "That was the most tiring experience I've gone through. I was finding myself getting a little short with some of the people I was working with and I was finding I was not looking forward to the next stop or the next meeting as much as I normally do."

Following two more gruelling days of campaigning in the interior of the province, Vander Zalm was persuaded to spend the weekend resting. David Poole joined the premier's tour for the remainder of the campaign to keep the road show on schedule and prevent the leader from flagging. Aside from the largely concealed physical toll, Vander Zalm's failure to settle the IWA strike did not hurt his campaign—in fact, he was given credit by many for at least trying to resolve the dispute. But now the tiring premier was increasingly castigated for having no policy, and for the final weeks of the campaign there were growing concerns about a government leader unprepared to discuss issues. Many remembered Kim Campbell's Whistler speech, in which she remarked "Charisma without substance is a dangerous thing." "Where's the beef?" shouted the occasional heckler. Bill Vander Zalm countered the criticism with his little-understood assertion that "style *is* substance."

B.C. politics is characterized by hard, real choices. In an era when apathetic voters complain that all politicians are alike and that political parties are indistinguishable once in office, British Columbia seems distinctively different. The polarization so tightly woven into the province's social fabric is highlighted and often exaggerated by the west coast politics of personality. The 1986 provincial election was a choice between a party with no policy and too much leader and a party with too much policy and no leader. Vander Zalm versus Skelly—a real choice, but virtually nobody considered it a genuine contest.

In the final week of the campaign a variety of factors conspired to produce a kind of uneasiness about an election that appeared to be sewn up far in advance of balloting day. On 17 October the U.S.

commerce department announced a preliminary ruling on the petition for a countervailing duty against Canadian lumber. While the recommended 15 per cent tariff was lower than many had expected, it was still a setback for many B.C. forest products manufacturers. But Vander Zalm downplayed the American announcement, saying it could have been worse and arguing that he now required a strong mandate to fight for a beneficial resolution of the countervail issue.

The weekend before polling day the premier was out on the hustings without Lillian. When asked where she was, Vander Zalm replied that she was at home scrubbing his socks. It was a statement which the fatigued premier quickly regretted, for it brought down a rain of invective from incensed women's groups; at subsequent rallies protesters threw socks at him. The sock-throwing was an obvious attempt at satire, but the premier strained to see the humour: "I ran out of socks and it becomes a national issue," he snapped.

Lastly, on the weekend before voting, a front-page headline in the Vancouver *Sun* read: "NDP Chops Socred Vote Lead." The story detailed the results of a province-wide poll which showed the gap between Social Credit and the NDP to be a mere five percentage points among decided voters. This was a far cry from polls published at the start of the campaign, which had suggested that the Socreds were in an eighteen point lead and heading for a possible sweep of the sixty-nine seats. The Vancouver *Sun* poll strengthened the Social Credit campaign, which was in danger of complacency, for it hammered home the need for organization on election day. The Social Credit campaign team could indeed feel the closing of the gap between themselves and the NDP, but they never felt they were in serious trouble. The *Sun* poll helped to lower expectations and get the party's vote out on election day.

On 20 October, two days before the B.C. election, Grant Devine's Tories were re-elected in a close fight with the NDP in Saskatchewan. For Vander Zalm this augured well for his own campaign, and he headed for the finish line with renewed vigour. During the last week of the campaign he boldly wrote down his prediction of the number of seats that Social Credit would win and sealed it in an envelope not to be opened until the polls closed on election night. He repeated this soothsaying with more than one media member.

On the day before voting, the premier gave a major substantive speech to a large audience at the Hotel Vancouver that was his personal response to charges that he was all style and no substance. It was one of the best addresses of his career, and it offered detailed commitments for his proposed Fresh Start. He spoke of instituting a consultative approach to governing, he promised reform of the legislature, and he talked about changes to the province's labour relations system which would usher in a new business and investment climate. He promised both a royal commission on education and improved postsecondary financial assistance. He spoke of privatizing public sector services and decentralizing government decision making. He said he would establish an economic development council to assist him in implementing a plan for a "new economy." In all it was an important policy statement, but it came at the wrong end of the election campaign.

Fears of voter complacency were washed away on 22 October by a 77 per cent voter turnout. The evening was anticlimactic; Whistler had been the real 1986 B.C. election, and this night would be a simple confirmation of change, a formal, democratic endorsement of a new guard already in place. Also responsible for the subdued atmosphere awaiting the Social Credit victory was the new party leader's dominant role in the election campaign: it was difficult for others to share in what was essentially a one-man victory.

BCTV declared a Social Credit majority only seventeen minutes after the polls closed. The Socreds received 49.7 per cent of the popular vote, compared to the NDP's 42.2 per cent. It appeared that the government party would control forty-nine of the sixty-nine seats, with the remaining twenty going to the NDP. The Liberals and other third parties were once more shut out. If not quite a landslide, it was the largest B.C. majority in many years. And the turnover in membership in the House was the largest ever, with a clear majority of the MLAs serving their first terms. Vander Zalm's promised Fresh Start would include fresh faces from the leadership race, including Mel Couvelier, Bud Smith and Kim Campbell. The NDP side of the House was also strongly rejuvenated with several promising new MLAs, including Vancouver mayor Mike Harcourt.

In many individual races, only a handful of votes separated candidates, and the inevitable recounts took place. Perhaps the most symbolic turnover occurred in the dual-member riding of Vancouver—Point Grey, where Kim Campbell had topped the polls. The recount saw the defeat of her running mate, long-time Socred cabinet minister and former Liberal leader Pat McGeer. The old guard was definitely giving way to a new guard. After the recounts, the standings were Social Credit forty-seven, NDP twenty-two. The number the premier had scribbled down and sealed until election night was forty-seven.

In the ballroom of the Hotel Vancouver on election night, there was much less enthusiasm and jubilation than there had been at Whistler; for many in the party the provincial election was a foregone conclusion. For the premier, numb with exhaustion, it was time to acknowledge victory: "There's just one way to describe it. Faaantaastic!" Vander Zalm now looked forward to a short rest and the start of a new challenge.

CHAPTER 6

Style and Substance

With the 1986 election, the Socreds became the model of political succession in Canada. Less obvious was the achievement of this through renewal which was often confused and disorderly, a comedy of errors dependent more upon the forces of personality than upon rational plans. Premier Vander Zalm was victorious without policies, without a well-oiled machine, without an effective advertising program—certainly a tribute to the politics of personality. And although his party was uncomfortable during the campaign and frustrated by the lack of attention paid to issues or local candidates, it was also evident that the premier's popularity was chiefly responsible for Social Credit victories in many close contests. Vander Zalm therefore accomplished a feat that Bill Bennett had never achieved—electing candidates on his own coattails.

"Mr. Vander Zalm's personal charisma, which I didn't think was going to be quite so good as it is, turned out to be absolute money in the bank for our party," said Stephen Rogers. Rogers, who on the road to Whistler had said he could never work with Vander Zalm, was now, like so many others, changing his tune: "Those of us who sought the leadership really failed to realize that the man has enormous personal popularity beyond the little group that we were dealing with."

After a decade of public upheaval in Canada's Pacific province, voters were willing and eager to place their trust in a new leader. It was a situation that should have played directly into the hands of the official opposition, but instead Bill Vander Zalm assumed the mantle of unofficial opposition leader, undercutting Bob Skelly and the NDP and ushering in a new style of government characterized at first by little more than positive thinking and smiling optimism. The NDP had a much better organized, more sophisticated election machine, but they had the wrong leader, the wrong strategy and a demonstrated inability to read the public mood. Vander Zalm's victory can therefore be seen as the triumph of high touch over high tech. The image, appeal and touch of the new leader defeated the formidable organization of his opponents. "The people in B.C. wanted a Prince Charles—Princess Diana combination," said former cabinet minister Jim Nielsen. "Vander Zalm offered that impression. He's a very capable guy when it comes to charisma, salesmanship, charm. That's what they wanted. And there's nothing wrong with that."

If the Vander Zalm juggernaut was running out of steam in the final days of the campaign, it was probably a blessing in disguise. A larger, more sweeping mandate could have raised expectations far beyond the bounds of reason and neutered the established opposition party as well. As it was, the victory was impressive, and public expectations were very high. British Columbians wanted a different style of government, one that was useful but also took some risks. The inevitable blemishes and errors would have some compensations if they also aroused interest and enthusiasm and even caused laughter from time to time. In late 1986 Premier Vander Zalm was focussing attention on his upbeat and confident messages, and like a Canadian version of Ronald Reagan, the Great Communicator, he promised "to make British Columbia the greatest place in the whole wide world."

All of this may suggest that leadership is paramount to political philosophy in British Columbia. "Ideas matter," the premier later said. "I think philosophy is important. Philosophy really does, for a good part, determine the direction. But a philosophy without strong leadership which merits respect is nothing."

Premier Vander Zalm's leadership was certainly respected enough to give him an impressive electoral mandate, but doubts lingered—even amongst those who had voted for him—about his ability to serve as premier. In the film *Being There*, Peter Sellers played Chance, a dim-witted gardener who, through a series of mishaps and comical coincidences, becomes a potential candidate for the presidency of the United States. Mistaken for profundity and symbolic significance are Chance's simple beliefs about gardening, like: "As long as the roots are not severed, all is well, and all will be well in the garden." In British Columbia, following the 1986 election, some observers wondered if the province's new premier *cum* gardener was a phenomenon akin to Chance the gardener. "Does he really know what he is doing?" asked *Equity*, a Vancouver business magazine. Although he had displayed outstanding political talents in both his ascendancy to the Socred leadership and in his election triumph, the abilities required to win power are very different from those necessary to exercise it responsibly. Clearly, the debate over style versus substance will be at the heart of British Columbia politics for at least as long as the new premier remains on the scene.

Bill Vander Zalm spoke a lot about style, even though Lillian urged him not to, saying, "People won't know what you're talking about." Nevertheless, the premier argued that style *is* substance and was determined to prove it during the course of his stewardship of the province. He disagreed with the contention that the talents used to win power were substantially different from those needed to practise power. And he used an analogy close to his heart to explain why:

> I've always maintained in business that the first impression is the best impression. You'll never get a second chance to make a first impression. So do your best.
>
> I've also said that it's not so much what you've got to sell. People can compete very easily in selling shrubs and bulbs because they basically come from the same source. You can compete with price, but only for so long, and then you're going to find out that you're going in the hole. But where you can beat your competition is in style. Do it classy. If you've got a garden centre, keep a clean store. It's the way you present your plants, it's the colour, it's the cleanliness, it's the way you approach your customer. It's *style*.
>
> Now, when you're out campaigning, it's style too. A bit of flair. Something that catches the audience and has some impact. If you're going to be a success campaigning, it's got to be done in style.
>
> And when you're running a premier's office or running a govern-

ment, sure there has to be a lot of substance. But substance without style? That won't get you anywhere. You can have the best shrubs in the world, but if you bury them or display them on a garbage heap, you're not going to sell them.

At Whistler, to promote a spirit of party unity, Bill Bennett had proclaimed of his successor: "I know that he can run a government." But many Socreds who had been close to Bennett harboured grave doubts. Patrick Kinsella said:

I believe Bill Vander Zalm's a one-term premier. I'm not sure he'll last a term. I think at some period he'll pack it in, because what Bill Bennett thrived on, the day-to-day dynamic of being premier, with all its ups and downs, is not something that Vander Zalm has the capacity for.

What he needs is a 365-day election writ every year—and then Bill Vander Zalm will prevail until the next century. But at some point reality seeps in—After all the hullabaloo and all the electioneering, what are you going to do for us, Mr. Premier? That's where Bill Vander Zalm will fail the test.

Such doubts were derived in large part from Vander Zalm's reputation for controversy and confrontation. The new premier, however, was determined to prove the doubters wrong, and he would in fact surprise most observers by waltzing through his first months in office in a steady and confident manner. Indeed, ever since he had announced his candidacy for the leadership, his moves were calm, collected and unfailingly on target. Pursuing his instincts, he committed few obvious errors and exercised political judgement far more mature than anyone had expected. And behind the scenes he was furiously developing a plan for dramatic provincial development, a new vision of the Good Life.

For a while it had appeared that the premier had no plan. This was true in the sense that he had surprised even himself by winning the party leadership, and he had not been fully prepared to assume office. In truth, Vander Zalm had a wealth of experience in public life, and he had strong views about the direction that public policy in British Columbia should take. He needed time, however, to assemble the details of this vision into a workable plan. Those who argued that he had a secret agenda were wrong, as were those

who argued that he had no agenda. Nevertheless, for a few months
after the election it seemed that British Columbia had entered a
new age of "agenda gap," where the government simply responded to the issues of the moment without a blueprint for an
ideological or political future.

For some this was an exhilarating experience, a clear departure
from the past when a Bill Bennett, a Dave Barrett or a W. A. C.
Bennett had directed the provincial agenda without brooking any
interference with their own well-laid plans. For others this was a
disappointment in that Vander Zalm had raised expectations which
showed no signs of immediate fulfilment. The author of the
"charisma without substance" statement, Kim Campbell, had
never been a particular fan of Bill Vander Zalm's. Now, however,
as a member of his team, she said: "I have to respect the fact that
Bill Vander Zalm has his own agenda of what he wants to accomplish, and it may not be what I want to accomplish. He wants to
change the tone of things. I think he has a view of wanting to
simplify government, and he's not afraid of that challenge."

Two weeks after his election, Bill Vander Zalm announced his
eighteen-member cabinet. At the swearing-in ceremony he described that cabinet as "a bright new chapter in the history of government in British Columbia," adding: "I'd like to emphasize
there's a lot of substance behind our new style and approach."

The cabinet included five rookie MLAs—Mel Couvelier, Peter
Dueck, Lyall Hanson, Stan Hagen and John Savage—and only six
holdovers from Bill Bennett's executive council. Stephen Rogers
made a surprise comeback into cabinet ranks, as did another
leadership candidate, Cliff Michael. Mel Couvelier, also a leadership contender, broke into cabinet in the important post of Finance. Vander Zalm was able to relinquish his position as minister
of finance not only because the work load would be too much for
one person but also because of his own growing confidence as
leader. "That safety valve was no longer required," he said. "I felt
secure."

His security was bolstered by the reshaping of his cabinet team.
Aside from Grace McCarthy, no other ministers hailed from the
class of '75, when Vander Zalm had first been appointed to the provincial cabinet. The retirement and electoral defeat of members of
the previous administration now helped to complete the process of
renewal, the second phase of the changing of the guard. Former

members of Bill Bennett's cabinet who were re-elected but not invited to re-enter cabinet included Austin Pelton, Alex Fraser and Russ Fraser. Another, Jim Hewitt, said: "Remember, I was one of the cabinet ministers he deemed gutless before he quit politics."

Three other MLAs who had sought the Socred leadership did not make it into Vander Zalm's cabinet: John Reynolds was nominated Speaker of the Legislative Assembly, and two bright newcomers— Bud Smith and Kim Campbell—were seen as Bennett's protégés, and were therefore not surprised to learn of their exclusion from cabinet, although many observers found it remarkable that the premier would pass over Bud Smith after his momentous crossing of the convention floor.

At the time his cabinet was sworn in, the premier characteristically stole the headlines from his newly appointed ministers by issuing a thirty-two-page paper on government reorganization, the first stage of his simplification program. The ministries of Consumer and Corporate Affairs and International Trade, Science and Investment were eliminated, and each new minister was given a detailed agenda which outlined public policy priorities and included deadlines for implementation. It was an unprecedented way to grab the reins of power.

During this early part of his mandate, the premier also had to consider the provincial bureaucracy. He strongly desired his Fresh Start to extend into the ranks of the civil service and indicated that a shuffle of deputy ministers—something unheard of—was on the horizon. He was not quick to reward those who had helped with his political resurrection, for he wanted to both ensure that he placed the right people in the right positions and, at the same time, prevent accusations of personal or political patronage. The only two appointments that could be so criticized were made at the end of the year, and they were both defensible. Vander Zalm's friend and former deputy minister Bill Long left the premier's office, where he was serving as a special adviser, and assumed the helm of the crown-owned B.C. Ferry Corporation. Former cabinet minister and Richmond MLA Jim Nielsen was appointed chairman of the Workers' Compensation Board. Other former ministers and Bennett loyalists waited in vain, if they waited at all, for calls from the new premier.

When it came to his own office, Vander Zalm was even more cautious. He was uncertain about the necessary staffing requirements but quite sure of what he did not want: any reminders of his predecessor. The premier's office under Bill Bennett had been such a strong symbol of disaffection with the old guard that Vander Zalm deliberately organized his affairs differently. Principal secretary Jerry Lampert had an agreement with the premier that he would leave Victoria shortly after the election, and it was assumed that David Poole would move from his position as executive director of the Social Credit Party to replace Lampert. Poole had built up a strong personal rapport with Vander Zalm during the election campaign, but the move to his new role was not the result of a joint decision.

> Towards the end of the campaign, at a Vancouver airport terminal, the premier pulled me to one side over by some vending machines and said: "Jerry's leaving, and I guess you sort of might come over and do that." And that was it. The day after the election he announced it at a press conference—that Jerry's leaving, that I would be taking his place. There was never any discussion. And as we came over to Victoria the next day, he said to me: "What does a principal secretary do, anyway?"

That there was no discussion, Poole said, ties in to the premier's philosophy that "this is all governed by someone else. We're just players in the game."

Poole became the most powerful nonelected government officer in British Columbia. In time, both he and his boss would have to come to terms with a perhaps unavoidable centralization of power in their office, in many respects reminiscent of the Bennett years. But during the months following the election, there could be no doubt that a fresh, new government was in place in Victoria. The Vander Zalm administration did not consider itself bound by any decisions of the previous government, even if there were a few holdovers from the Bennett regime. One long-time deputy minister confided that the change in direction was greater than that experienced in Victoria when the NDP had defeated W. A. C.'s Socreds in 1972. A striking example of this occurred in the summer of 1987 when it was revealed that the first phase of the Coquihalla highway, which had been "fast-tracked" to completion prior to Bill Bennett's retirement, had cost almost $160 million more than the forecasted $250 million. Such a massive cost overrun on a high-profile megaproject was decried by many as a major scandal. Vander Zalm responded not by defending his predecessor's pet project but by ordering a special commission of enquiry into spending on the Coquihalla. It was the reaction one might have expected from a government that had uncovered a secret left behind by the political opposition.

This political reshaping of British Columbia was favourably received. The only danger evident during Vander Zalm's extended honeymoon with the public was the threat of over-expectation. When hopes are so high, the prospects for disappointment and disillusionment are usually higher still, and some ministers feared that the public might expect more than the government would be able to give.

One person who never considered such a possibility was the province's greatest exponent of the power of positive thinking, Bill Vander Zalm. With his new cabinet in place, his office installed and the province adjusting to life under new leadership, the premier began to unwind his vision. His background as a small entrepreneur shaped his views about the continued development of British Columbia. Many had supported Vander Zalm as a best bet for a nostalgic return to the Good Life, but for those waiting for things to get back to normal in British Columbia, the bad news was that there was no "normal" to get back to. The world had changed, and British Columbia's cornucopia of natural resources was no longer a guarantee of wealth and prosperity.

The good news was that the province was slowly but surely diversifying its economic base and learning to compete in the world marketplace. Vander Zalm was anxious to use his new-found powers as building blocks for a new era. In many respects his ideas were a natural outgrowth of the economic policies of the Bennett years. Restraint and the shrinking of government in the early 1980s were indispensable elements of economic recovery, but while Premier Vander Zalm never quarrelled with these hotly pursued goals of Bill Bennett's regime, he disagreed with the techniques:

There was no alternative. If they hadn't introduced restraint, we'd be worse off today. As it is, we've got horrendous deficits. So we paid, during restraint, for too much extravagance in prior years. But it had to be done.

Where the government went wrong was not in its program but in its inability to sell the program. And that was so obvious, seeing it from the outside. They weren't selling the message properly. It was confrontational. Fighting in the streets. Solidarity versus the government. The government finally won out, but the image came to be one of confrontation and fighting.

Vander Zalm not only wanted to accelerate the reduction of government's size and scope but also desired to encourage more than ever before a true diversification of the provincial economy. The economic growth of the 1950s and 1960s, which led to the rapid industrialization of British Columbia, had been followed by economic instability during the 1970s and a deep recession in the early 1980s. The province's economy suffered through a painful deindustrialization. Continuing change in the mid-1980s led Vander Zalm to preach a post-recession economic vision of reindustrialization.

It was an appealing, simplistic view of a developing empire of stable, diversified, B.C.-owned businesses. Some of its key elements included decentralization of government services, an emphasis on tourist industries, and developing the province's universities to attract technology industries. This was no standard political or corporate response to a retrenching world economy; it was more a radical vision of economic change from the "small is beautiful" school. It was a vision that Bill Vander Zalm would have to sell—and he would have to market it more effectively than his predecessor had sold restraint.

"I will work a whole lot harder to get fifty businesses employing twenty people each than one business employing a thousand people," he said.

There are a lot of available resources in communities, and if we can create fifty or a hundred jobs, it will have a big impact. And that's where a lot of the future has to be. It's a changing economy. We're going from the megaproject and the historical resource-based industries to a lot of little cottage-type industries that will provide stable jobs and diversification.

There is nothing complicated in Vander Zalm's vision for economic development; however, its realization would not be without complications. Nevertheless, during his first months in office, even larger controversies affecting the province and its major industries would be resolved in a manner which the premier could call successful. For example, the dispute over the American petition for a countervailing duty against Canadian lumber could have been disastrous for a fledgling B.C. government. Shortly after becoming premier, Vander Zalm stated that the province's forest stumpage fees should be reviewed. This prospect caused considerable concern amongst some of the large forest companies; it was also an important change of direction for the B.C. government, which under Bill Bennett had refused to waver in the face of American claims that low stumpage rates constituted a subsidy to the province's forest industry.

The countervailing duty was fraught with economic and political complexities which required delicate diplomacy between provincial and national governments. Rather than fight the battle through the American legal system, Vander Zalm argued for a negotiated settlement with the Americans. His viewpoint prevailed, and the settlement, achieved at the last possible moment on New Year's Eve 1986, saw a 15 per cent Canadian export tax imposed on softwood lumber entering the United States.

It was a difficult, contentious resolution. On the one hand, Vander Zalm could take credit for expediting a negotiated settlement which would see a 15 per cent industry levy remain in Canada, bringing approximately $350 million a year to the cash-starved provincial treasury. On the other hand, critics of the settlement argued that it represented a loss of national sovereignty and that Canadian negotiators should never have made a deal but should have fought the American petition to the bitter end.

Some industry critics, particularly those associated with the trade associations dominated by large, integrated forest companies, were especially incensed by the agreement. Adam Zimmerman, chairman of MacMillan Bloedel and head of the Canadian Forest Industries Council, was outraged that the final negotiations had excluded business bosses such as himself. He suggested that a timber treaty negotiated by politicians and bureaucrats was akin to a hospital orderly performing brain surgery. Such comments drove a thick wedge between big business interests and the Vander Zalm administration. The populist premier was not uncomfortable with this wedge, and he only smiled when Zimmerman asserted: "The premier has got to learn that international commodity markets don't work the same way that local businesses do."

There was no doubt that Bill Vander Zalm represented the interests of British Columbia better and more completely than Adam Zimmerman. The premier kept in touch with the public not by polls and sophisticated public opinion research but by constant contact with people. He loved to mingle and talk with people, lunging into crowds wherever he went, eager to listen to the wishes and concerns of anyone he could meet. For Vander Zalm these random samplings of public opinion were more valuable than expensive commissioned polls. To ensure that he remained plugged in to the public mood, he regularly held "town hall" style meetings in communities throughout the province. He also took the unprecedented step of hosting a monthly, province-wide radio phone-in show to solicit opinions on government policy.

"Communications is politics, and politics is politicking," said Vander Zalm. He believed that communicating directly with the people of his province was good politics. The only danger inherent in his constant politicking was that it focussed attention as never before on the government leader. He appropriated most issues for himself, giving the strong impression of a one-man government. Members of his cabinet typically stood in his shadow: during the countervail case, little was heard from the minister of forests; during the IWA labour dispute, there was no evidence of a minister of labour. In time, though, he would be forced to come to terms with the critical concepts of cabinet government, team building and delegation of power and authority.

Premier Vander Zalm ended 1986 on a high note; his honeymoon with British Columbians was still in bloom, and his pace showed no signs of slowing. In the New Year, however, he would contend with growing concerns about the shape and direction of public policy. The public would have to wait until the administration's first legislative session to acquire a true sense of where Vander Zalm wished to lead the province. A few issues crept into public view, offering fugitive glimpses of Vander Zalm's character and hints of a highly personalized approach to public administration. To be sure, the premier was concerned with economic issues, the provincial deficit and promoting a business orientation for government programs, but his new style of leadership also focussed on social matters in a way never before experienced in the province. Perhaps the most controversial aspect of the political reshaping of British Columbia was this new emphasis on moral issues.

During the election campaign and afterward, Premier Vander Zalm had spoken freely and fervently about prostitution, abortion and sex education. His Catholic background dictated strong views that he was unafraid to express publicly. Most politicians steer clear of such heated issues, which usually bear no relationship to party line support and yet hold the potential to alienate many voters. Vander Zalm, however, spoke openly of his desire to see fewer abortions performed in B.C. hospitals, and he railed against government funding of sex education in public schools, arguing that such programs promoted promiscuity. In April of 1987, in one of his daring exercises in instant accessibility, he invited reporters into his office to watch him watch a controversial AIDS video proposed for viewing in Vancouver high schools. At the conclusion of the eighteen-minute film, the premier firmly condemned the production as the world's "longest-running condom ad." And he summed up its message as: "I want to have sex, but I don't want to die."

In a modern, increasingly pluralistic society such as British Columbia's, such issues are not the usual fodder for politicians, but Vander Zalm believes he has an obligation to make his views known; he instinctively feels that citizens want to know what their leader's character is made from, and he senses that moral issues are ultimately more important than economic concerns as we head towards the conclusion of the twentieth century.

I personally believe that moral issues are perhaps more important than whether we build Site C on the Peace River or build a new highway or finish the Coquihalla. I think all of these kinds of moral issues in the end will structure the way we go and what happens. That's not to say that I could ever hope to change the views on abortion or to come exactly to the way that I might like to see it go. But I think I can be a leader in the sense that we need to keep things at least defensible for the majority of the people. There has to be a lot of pressure put on because otherwise it will sooner or later just run away on us. I believe that I have that responsibility.

We tend to think of people as being very much one way or the other on these issues. Whereas probably the majority of the people, in their hearts, are somewhere in between. They don't want too much of one or too much of the other. I don't believe that the majority of British Columbians—good, honest, hard-working individuals —really want wide open abortions, for instance. They probably wouldn't go out there and fight against it because they don't feel that strongly or they're not that much involved. But in their hearts they wouldn't want to see it wide open. That's my own gut feel. My sense. And I think those people are really looking for someone who says: "Hey, there's got to be a brake put on some of these things."

A leader should speak out on these issues even though they may be controversial. I think it gives people a sense of security to know reasonably well where their leaders are taking them. And they feel safer if someone expresses a concern about these sorts of issues.

Naturally, Bill Vander Zalm was criticized for his stances on such personal matters. He was accused by some of intolerance and of imposing his own moral standards on the community. "Don't Play High Priest Role, Bill!" editorialized the Vancouver *Province*. But the premier could not restrain himself from speaking out. "I think people elect others to represent them basically on what they stand for, which includes, certainly, their moral values," he said. And he took both delight and comfort in the different style of leadership he provided, rarely seen in the cautious, conservative world of Canadian politics. Motivated by his formidable intuition —his "gut feel"—Vander Zalm sensed he could afford to take risks with moral issues. He developed a feeling of political invulnerability on these issues and believed that a changing mood in society allowed for and even encouraged this brand of leadership.

There are more and more people concerned less and less with "What's in it for me?" This "me" thing, which was eating up the world, is changing. I think we're at the beginning of a new view where people are becoming more concerned about the—for lack of a better word—spiritual side of life. Maybe, in part, my stance on some of these moral issues fits in with this changing theme as well.

Undaunted by the challenge, the premier was determined to push the province forward into the new age he felt was dawning. He believed he was the right leader at the right time, perhaps chosen by some higher authority to help change the established order of things for the better.

The Vander Zalm administration's first speech from the throne in March 1987 was an innovative address outlining an array of ambitious new approaches to public policy. It contained no mention of megaprojects—no dams, no highways, no edifices of any sort. It specifically referred to a need for social reform—reducing the abortion rate, increasing welfare spending, increasing educational funding, reforming the province's labour laws and launching an aggressive new privatization program. "Job one is to get the government off the back and out of the way of the private sector," said the speech. "We have a plan for a new economy—we will make it work." These policy directions bore the unmistakable stamp of the premier: they were upbeat in tone and hugely ambitious.

Ten days after the legislative session commenced, Minister of Finance Mel Couvelier brought down the government's first budget, an unusual document providing a mixed bag of economic policy and tax reform and—if any further evidence was needed— concrete proof that this was a government uncommitted to the status quo. The word *restraint* was not uttered a single time in Couvelier's budget address, which did, however, contain the following statement: "If British Columbia is to achieve its full potential, we cannot rely on past solutions to tide us over until normal times return."

The budget speech may have been read by the finance minister, but there was no denying the premier's authorship. In a significant departure from the economic strategy of the previous Socred regime, the record $10 billion budget raised taxes to aid social programs, increased welfare rates, increased education spending, cut the provincial sales tax by 1 per cent, raised income taxes and eliminated a nuisance tax on restaurant meals. Two measures caused serious disenchantment, even amongst Socred supporters: a tax on the sale of real estate and a fee on prescription drugs for senior citizens. Although fiscally conservative, the budget was tempered with a social conscience; parts could have been written by a left-wing government, with its theme of "Investing in People." After being subjected to the cold light of scrutiny, it was difficult to determine the budget's overall philosophy or guiding principle.

Premier Vander Zalm was disappointed that his populist budget was not better received. He considered it "fairly daring" and at the same time generous. He had also wanted to deliver some good news and positive direction to soften the mood of the public before he proceeded with what he knew would be a highly contentious legislative program.

In the premier's mind it was a foregone conclusion that the first legislative session would be dominated by labour issues. The process had started with his failed mediation of the IWA–forest industry dispute during the election campaign. "There's got to be a better way," he said at the time. He was determined to prevent long labour disputes from further damaging British Columbia's economy and its reputation abroad, and he asked senior public servants to begin preparing options for legislative action. Then, following the election, he sent his new labour minister, Lyall Hanson, on a province-wide round of public hearings on labour law reform. The premier had some definite ideas of his own, which would be combined with the recommendations of his cabinet and public servants and input from Hanson's labour review, to form the most explosive legislative package since the Bennett government's restraint program. Several officials within the government urged the premier to go slowly, to make a few changes over a few years. But Vander Zalm responded: "We know what it is we want to see accomplished. We know how it is we want to see it done. We better do it all at once."

It was Vander Zalm's determination to break free from what he called the "tyranny of the experts" that resulted in the tabling of the complex and sweeping Bill 19—the Industrial Relations Reform Act—and Bill 20—the Teaching Profession Act. Bill 19 proposed to extensively amend the province's thirteen-year-old Labour Code and create an administrative framework for collective bargaining and the resolution of labour disputes. An Industrial Relations Council was to replace the Labour Relations Board, with the new tribunal to be headed by Ed Peck, the Bennett government's czar of restraint. Bill 20 created a professional College of Teachers and allowed teachers to form local unions for collective bargaining. Vander Zalm emphasized his view that the two bills would increase workplace democracy and protect the "third party" in labour disputes—the public interest.

Labour issues have always been at the centre of politics in Canada's most unionized province, and organized labour responded to these radical reforms at first with apprehension and later with loud protests and job action that brought the Vander Zalm government's Fresh Start back into line with the hard-core reality of west coast politics.

In many respects the heated debates and near-violent rhetoric that consumed British Columbia in the spring and summer months of 1987 were a response to technically complex, little-understood legislation. Although few representatives of organized labour would admit it, the legislative package could have been far more restrictive to their historic powers of bargaining and organization. Indeed, many union professionals had feared that Vander Zalm would introduce right-to-work laws which would have seriously undermined the legitimacy of trade unions in British Columbia. Furthermore, many representatives of the business community were not comfortable with the new era in industrial relations. Jim Matkin of the B.C. Business Council, for instance, was an early critic of the government's far-reaching reforms.

Prior to the legislative session, the B.C. Business Council, the B.C. Federation of Labour and other business groups had joined forces to launch the Pacific Institute on Industrial Policy, which was billed as a co-operative effort to promote labour harmony. Yet it was more an attempt to dissuade Vander Zalm from undertaking any precipitous action which might rock the established foundation of industrial relations. As the new head of the B.C. Federation of Labour, Ken Georgetti, said: "I don't think the premier has realized how much he had motivated the parties to change themselves. It's more the fear." The introduction of Bills 19 and 20 caused the disintegration of the Pacific Institute on Industrial Policy and other institutional efforts to find labour-management peace.

Premier Vander Zalm was determined to shake up the fraternity of B.C. industrial relations experts who worked in an incestuous private world which sometimes ignored the reality of working life in British Columbia. A generation of labour lawyers, consultants, union leaders, corporate industrial relations officers and industry association chiefs had built up a system which often failed the test of effectiveness or efficiency and did little more than provide comfortable salaries and benefits for a protected class of professionals. Virtually all of these established groups would now howl in a rage at the new government's ingenuous attempt to transcend the problems and sins of the past. Both Bills 19 and 20 were undoubtedly prepared in haste and were marked by imperfections in drafting and in meaning—they would need to be broadly amended before becoming law. But the demands of the special interest groups to withdraw both bills only increased the premier's resolve to see them passed into the province's statute books.

Bill Vander Zalm believed that for the British Columbia Teachers Federation (BCTF) to serve as both a quasi trade union as well as a professional disciplinary body represented a conflict of interest. Recent highly publicized cases of sexual abuse of students by teachers in British Columbia had demonstrated a need to strengthen professional and ethical standards. Vander Zalm's response was to create the College of Teachers, controlled by teachers, which would deal with matters of teacher certification, and to give teachers in each school district the option of establishing unions. Certainly this was a challenge to the authority and supremacy of the BCTF, but the bill also gave teachers the right to form unions, the right to strike and the right to bargain collectively for working conditions. The BCTF held that Bill 20 was anti-teacher and that the premier was fixed on destroying their organization. The bill brought forward charges that it was "the most vicious, the most monstrous, the most insidious attack upon the teaching profession ever perpetuated in the history of education in this country." The teachers, in the past a formidable political force in British Columbia shut down most public schools in the province for one day to protest the legislation. Furthermore, the BCTF asked teachers to refuse to supervise extracurricular school activities for the remainder of the school year. However, such actions discredited the BCTF in the eyes of the public.

After introducing substantive amendments to Bill 20, and after the teachers' walkout, Premier Vander Zalm, in a letter to the province's daily newspapers, explained his refusal to withdraw the legislation:

In a democracy, all citizens have the right to choose by majority vote the government that will make the laws. It is critical that we not allow that system to be damaged or destroyed by turning majority against minority or minority against majority. It is the prerogative of government to introduce legislation, and those opposed to the government have the inalienable right to express their opposition to the

legislation . . . but not to act illegally. Government cannot and must
not respond to illegal acts. . . . And as a duly elected government
we are not prepared to capitulate. There is no need, no reason, no
benefit for teachers to use students by denying them otherwise regular activities in order to fight government simply because they are
not getting everything exactly as they would want.

The battle against Bill 19 was more protracted and ultimately
took the bloom off Bill Vander Zalm's image as a new man. The
fresh start characterized by co-operation was now being replaced
by confrontation. It was a far cry from the protests and violence associated with the Bennett government's restraint program, but the
rhetoric was often as heated. The labour movement called Bill 19
"draconian"; Shirley Carr, president of the Canadian Labour Con-
gress, speaking to a union meeting in Vancouver, accused Vander
Zalm of "economic terrorism" and added, "As a new Canadian citizen you have no right to bring your right-wing fascist ideas into
this democratic country."

Although trade union leaders differed about how to deal with the
government's labour legislation, Ken Georgetti did his level best
to remain cool, calm and moderate. The struggles over Bill 19 provided this young, new-guard labour leader with an invaluable education in B.C. politics. But he was no match for the determined,
vastly more experienced Bill Vander Zalm who, while admitting
that his legislation was less than perfect, again refused to back
down. He said his government would accept recommendations for
specific amendments to Bill 19, but would not waver from the
basic principles it advanced; indeed, Labour Minister Lyall
Hanson introduced almost fifty changes to the complex law.

Inside the legislature, opposition labour critic Colin Gabelmann
thoroughly and responsibly debated the principles and details of
Bill 19. Outside the House, organized labour mounted an expensive advertising and media campaign of protest. They were
joined by former deputy minister of labour Graham Leslie, who
had left the government before the legislation was introduced. He
referred to Bill 19 as an "act of legislative violence" and said it had
been drafted by "too few and too narrow minds."

The problem with Bill 19 was that it was simply too complicated
to be understood by most British Columbians. It consisted of a
hundred changes to many elements of existing provincial labour

law, with no single identifying characteristic other than the possibility of intervention in labour disputes that threatened the public interest. The main objections to Bill 19 were to the wide-ranging powers it conferred on the head of the new Industrial Relations Council. The government offered amendments to soften these powers, but would not withdraw Bill 19 or refer it to a committee. This intransigence resulted in a showdown with the B.C. Federation of Labour. On 1 June a general strike by at least 200,000 union members closed down business in much of British Columbia.

The general strike showed the province to be bitterly polarized, with the unions able to mobilize enough support to prove their points and flex their muscles. At first it seemed that the government, though stubborn, was still widely respected by most British Columbians for staying on its course. In a democracy, after all, economic disruption is not the appropriate response of a group that loses an argument or an election. However, Attorney General Brian Smith was able to snatch defeat from the jaws of victory by filing an application for an injunction in the Supreme Court of B.C. that would ban the B.C. Federation of Labour or any other group from taking actions such as general strikes. The attorney general's application referred to an illegal conspiracy on the part of union leaders, suggesting that they were guilty of sedition and of trying to overthrow an elected government.

The application for an injunction was seen as an overreaction, a paranoid effort which further incited opponents of the government's labour legislation. "We won the battle and lost the war," confided one prominent Socred. The premier publicly rebuked his attorney general and told reporters he was not even sure what the word *sedition* meant. The application, which was eventually thrown out of court, was an embarrassment for the Vander Zalm administration; it would have been politically safer to offer no formal response to the general strike.

The confrontational action was viewed as a botched attempt to muzzle opponents of the government. As such it signalled a turning point in the legislative session, raising questions about the direction of the Vander Zalm government and the premier's control over his cabinet. Perhaps Vander Zalm was "winging it" too much and now needed to enforce discipline on both himself and his cabinet. He certainly had to take a hard look at communications problems which were difficult to control. A reservoir of good will towards Bill Vander Zalm still existed, but it was slowly being drained. The voices of his critics were growing louder, and the silence amongst his supporters was sometimes deafening as well.

Although union leaders threatened to continue their protests, there were no more general strikes. Eventually the amended versions of Bills 19 and 20 were passed by the legislature; the premier indicated that he would withhold proclamation of certain controversial sections of Bill 19—those dealing with the intervention of cabinet or the legislature in labour disputes and the appointment of special mediators—proclaiming them only if it became necessary. However, the B.C. Federation of Labour and other non-affiliated unions announced that they would boycott the new industrial relations tribunal, making the government's system difficult to operate, if not unworkable in the short term. In addition, the unions launched legal action against the government, holding that the new labour laws were unconstitutional. Clearly, labour issues were going to be a source of controversy well beyond Bill Vander Zalm's first legislative session, chiefly because industrial relations are rather like sexual relations—they're better between two consenting parties.

In the midst of these labour wars, the political reshaping of British Columbia resolutely proceeded. It was clear that Bob Skelly could not continue to lead the NDP; the daggers were drawn within his party on election night, when he was personally blamed for the party's defeat. Indeed, the Toronto *Globe and Mail* dubbed him Canada's "worst politician" of 1986. It was later revealed that, even prior to the election, a number of NDP MLAs, recognizing that Skelly was no match for the popular Vander Zalm, had voted for a leadership review. However, a change of leadership on the verge of an election campaign was simply not practical for the NDP—a happy coincidence for the Socreds.

The remarkable facts about Skelly are that a person of his temperament was able to win the leadership of a political party hoping to form a government and that he was able to serve as leader of the official opposition for two years without anyone, including the normally aggressive B.C. news media, taking a hard look at his obvious weaknesses.

During the election, many who witnessed his trembling hands

and quavering voice wondered why this man was in politics. It was
like a person who was deathly afraid of saws had decided to become a carpenter. When Skelly resigned as NDP leader, he described his nervousness and speech anxiety as an affliction common
amongst politicians and said "some take tranquilizers, some take
whatever else they take, some take booze." He was then forced to
publicly apologize to other MLAs for his remarks about drug abuse,
tacitly recognizing that his was a special fear. Graham Lea, who
had served as his caucus colleague for many years, said he could
never understand Skelly. When it came Skelly's turn to speak in
the House, his colleagues would look for him, only to find he had
gone home. Said Lea: "My wife, Sharon, was working in the
caucus. One time Skelly had to speak, and he was rushing through
the caucus office looking for Valium. And so Sharon said, 'I have
one.' Skelly said, 'One? Four!' Down the hatch."

Having lost four consecutive elections after the single victory in
half a century, British Columbia's socialist party had come to believe it was destined to serve as the perpetual party of opposition.
They had a formidable party organization and a strong base of support, but invariably their election campaigns were characterized by
misguided strategy. Also, the NDP wanted to correct past grievances rather than move confidently towards the future.

The trauma of the election defeat needed to be exorcized
quickly, and a leadership convention was called for April of 1987.
Mike Harcourt immediately emerged as the leading candidate. For
a short while it appeared that some of British Columbia's federal
New Democrats might contest the provincial leadership; even the
blustery head of the IWA, Jack Munro, mulled over a run at the
job. However, it was soon accepted that Harcourt was the party's
best bet, although some NDP members were dismayed that they
could field only one credible candidate to succeed Bob Skelly.

Described by one newspaper as a "relentlessly amiable moderate," Mike Harcourt was crowned leader of the NDP by acclamation on 12 April 1987. He launched his leadership by counting
down the "thousand days" until the next election. To the backdrop of heated protests over the government's labour legislation,
Harcourt presented himself as a moderate, sane, safe choice compared with the radical Vander Zalm approach. Harcourt's primary
challenge was to maintain public interest in the NDP as a realistic

alternative to Social Credit. Certainly he was a very different kind of politician than Premier Vander Zalm—just as the NDP leadership succession was a study in contrasts with the Socred experience at Whistler. There was, in fact, no comparison between the two events, as Harcourt later said:

> First of all, our convention was not there for media hoopla. There were not twelve people down in the gladiator pit bloodying each other and making it exciting for the commentators and the media. Their leadership convention was taking place two or three months prior to an election. That's when you want to generate interest and excitement. Ours took place three years before an election, so there was no need to build up that hoopla.
>
> Secondly, there were some very serious splits within the Social Credit Party about where they should be going and who would be their leader. And that showed up in all the people who were running. In our party there was tremendous unanimity about what needed to be done, and I was seen to be the right person at the right time to do it—to change the tone, the attitude and the approach of the New Democratic Party.

Mike Harcourt wanted to take his party's tone from downbeat to upbeat; the attitude he wanted to instill was one that looked toward winning the next election, rather than focus on aimless Socred-bashing; and his approach was to tell British Columbians what his party stood for, not what the party was against. Harcourt is certainly no firebrand, but that could conceivably be to his great political advantage. Perhaps only in British Columbia's unique political culture could the NDP emerge as the party of moderation, but in a period of national ascendancy for the NDP, Mike Harcourt —low-key, nonthreatening, experienced, a winner—is perhaps the perfect leader of a rejuvenating provincial party. And he takes great delight in pointing out the differences between himself and the premier: "In very simple terms, it's Moderate Mike versus Radical Bill."

Moderate Mike is also a fascinated observer of Bill Vander Zalm.

> People underestimate him if they don't realize that he's a very good salesman of the Bill Vander Zalm persona. He's perfected the sell-

ing of Bill Vander Zalm. He's not a charismatic politician; I think
that's a misuse of the word. But he's a very good salesman of Bill
Vander Zalm. People sometimes underestimate that quality.

But you shouldn't overestimate him either, because he has two
very large Achilles' heels. One is that he doesn't have an intellectual
grist to grind ideas through. That doesn't mean that he's not in-
telligent or he's not cunning or that he doesn't know how to strum
the strings of the populist harp. He can do that—that's part of his
salesmanship. But Vander Zalm doesn't rigorously work ideas
through. And that gets him into all sorts of difficulties because he
then has to rely on his own personal prejudice. He therefore misses
a whole bunch of fundamental points, such as keeping his personal
views separate from his public activities. There *is* a separation of
church and state. We *do* have pluralistic democracy, which means
you have to be tolerant of other viewpoints.

Mike Harcourt, playing the role of astute compromiser, proved a
formidable opponent for Bill Vander Zalm. A winner versus a winner—but as W. A. C. Bennett said, "In politics, only one can
succeed." The tables now turned on the politics of personality in
British Columbia. No longer could a Social Credit leader effectively invoke the paranoid style, as W. A. C. Bennett did when he
had warned that the socialist hordes were at the gates. The hordes
were now a tame lot led by a measured, likable fellow who, if not
inspiring, at least exuded confidence and competence. Counting
down his thousand days, Harcourt said of Vander Zalm: "I beat
him once and I'm looking forward to beating him again. If he's
there."

If he's there. Several close observers of the premier wondered
whether or not he would fight another election. For opponents of
Vander Zalm this may simply have been a wish that he might
somehow self-destruct; for others it had something to do with his
mercurial personality and unpredictable career. Many have found
Vander Zalm impossible to second guess. And the premier's principal secretary, David Poole, just coming to terms with his boss's
goal-oriented approach to life, said that for the premier, getting
there was the battle. "With Bill Vander Zalm the challenge is to be
doing it. It's not to have done it and to have won. If he suddenly
discovered it wasn't fun any more, he'd leave. There's no intrinsic
reward in it for him just to be premier."

There was no lack of opportunity for Bill Vander Zalm to keep himself and his government focussed on new challenges. He realized that his goal of reshaping British Columbia could not be achieved quickly or easily, and his private objective was to serve as premier for at least two terms before going "back to the garden." After a year in office, however, the premier looked tired, his hair was rapidly greying and he was visibly aging under the weight of the pressures, responsibilities and the gruelling pace he set for himself. When he first became premier, he had remarked that the job was a piece of cake. "I still say it's a piece of cake," he said almost a year later. "But I now qualify that by saying it's a hell of a big piece of cake. It consumes you totally, seven days a week. You have four hours of restful sleep a night and you pick up whatever little bit you can on airplanes when you're travelling. It's tremendously demanding. People talking to you, pressuring you, and demands being put on your head. Unless you can take all that, you could grow old very quickly."

By the time his government's first legislative session adjourned for the summer in July of 1987, Premier Vander Zalm had already made a lasting impression on his province. In addition to Bills 19 and 20, a variety of other reforms had been initiated, including reviews of education, forest management and the electoral system. The government itself had also been largely reshaped not only by virtue of a dramatically different style of leadership and new political management but also by a shake-up in the public service. In April the premier shuffled ten deputy ministers, most being moved to areas they had never held responsibility for. This unprecedented change was well received by the deputies, who relished the new challenges and appreciated the premier's confidence in their administrative abilities. But Vander Zalm was also criticized for this novel management technique because he had not consulted with his ministers before changing their senior officials. He justified his action by saying a deputy minister's first loyalties were to the government and the premier: "We are not concerned about what a minister likes. What is more important is the overall functioning and effectiveness of government." It was an attitude strangely reminiscent of Bill Bennett's.

The other major achievement of the four-and-a-half-month-long legislative session was that, in spite of a return to confrontational politics over Bills 19 and 20, the mood and decorum in the legisla-

tive assembly had markedly improved. The B.C. House had for
many years held an unsavoury reputation among Commonwealth
parliaments. At its best it was referred to as "The Zoo." At its
worst it was labelled irrelevant. Now, a new parliament dominated
by new members determined to make the legislative process work
in a dynamic but mannerly fashion. Mike Harcourt said: "The premier and I have worked very hard to ensure that the legislature is a
place that you can bring your relatives to and young children can
come in without having their ears covered."

The change in the legislature was reflected by a spirit of co-
operation amongst government and opposition MLAs who had no
illusion about the essence of the institution of parliament: it was a
civilized substitute for civil war. The elected representatives
fought with reasoned debate instead of with guns in the streets.
Premier Vander Zalm advanced the goals of legislative reform by
ensuring the passage of legislation to create a bipartisan board of
internal economy to oversee the independent administration of
legislative services and activities. He was moving more slowly,
however, in reactivating long-dormant legislative committees or
fulfilling his promise of instituting televised proceedings of House
debates.

During his first year as premier, Vander Zalm also played an important role on the national stage. While he continued the tradition
of strong regional leadership, giving vent to the unique alienation
sometimes suffered in British Columbia, he also credibly projected
an understanding and appreciation of a national interest. That is
not to say that he avoided disputes with the federal government;
indeed, that would be un-Canadian for a provincial premier. The
Vander Zalm administration scrapped with Ottawa over an over-
ruled effort to offer investors provincially guaranteed dividends
and tax deferrals in "trust units" for Vancouver's rapid transit system. Then there was a prolonged bout of squabbling over Victoria's attempt to have Vancouver recognized as an international
banking and financial centre. Such political differences were
countered by the formation of a unique provincial-federal council
of ministers designed to address disputes between the two levels
of government.

Vander Zalm's forays into the field of federal-provincial diplomacy had mixed results. In March of 1987 he was booed in Ottawa

by native leaders at the first ministers' conference on aboriginal self-government. The B.C. premier, along with other western premiers whose provinces would be most affected by a proposed constitutional entrenchment of native self-government, said he could not agree to a proposal which was not clearly defined and yet could have far-reaching implications for public administration in his province. One B.C. native leader called Bill Vander Zalm a racist. Metis leader Jim Sinclair said: "It's a shame that you can come here and in a few years become the premier of one of the largest provinces in Canada, and yet you will not recognize the rights of our people here in this country."

Generally, Premier Vander Zalm played a constructive role at federal-provincial meetings. With his positive attitude and a firm belief in the power of personality, he was prepared to ensure that British Columbia was well represented in the councils of confederation. In June of 1987, when the Meech Lake Accord was signed, officially bringing Quebec into the Canadian constitutional fold as a "distinct society," it was ironic to see Bill Vander Zalm playing the part of one of the new fathers of confederation, for as a cabinet minister he had sung songs about René Lévesque as a frog and had complained about bilingual Corn Flakes boxes. Indeed, it was Vander Zalm, late in an all-night negotiating session, who had reassured disgruntled Quebec premier Robert Bourassa, saying: "Don't worry. We'll settle this tonight." They did. (At the ratification ceremony the following day, the document was passed to Vander Zalm for signing by the senior federal government adviser, his old nemesis, Norman Spector.)

Bill Vander Zalm knew that to be respected in British Columbia he had to bargain hard with the federal government. This is the long-standing reality of Canadian federalism. In July 1987 the premier and prime minister signed the agreement that created South Moresby National Park in the Queen Charlotte Islands. The agreement, a controversial one which alienated the rights of resource industries in the area, contained substantially more benefits to British Columbia than the federal government had initially proposed. The $106 million package was hailed by many, including some conservationists, as a tribute to the premier's hard bargaining with the feds. At the signing ceremony in Victoria Vander Zalm said to Prime Minister Mulroney: "It just shows that when you mix several parts of Irish charm and Dutch stubbornness—pardon me, determination—and shake things up, good, positive things happen."

At the end of his first year as premier, Vander Zalm described his role on the national stage as a comfortable one but predicted that federal-provincial relations would be stormy for the remainder of his mandate.

> Despite the powers of Quebec and Ontario, I think we have a good opportunity to have the B.C. voice heard. There's a lot of respect for the B.C. position. But the big issue for the next number of years is going to be how do we address B.C.'s fair share in confederation? There's going to be a growing battle against all of the inequities that exist. That's going to be the big battle and I'm going to be as aggressive as anyone has ever been.

For Premier Vander Zalm, heading into his second year in power, privatization was the next important step in his revolutionary mandate. He was committed to reducing the size and complexity of government and saw the transfer of crown corporations to the private sector and the sale of other public-owned assets as an important stage in the process of remaking British Columbia. He described it as a big gamble but was prepared to go farther down the road of privatization than most observers realized, for he saw it as a way to both reduce the provincial debt and establish new industries in British Columbia. And he was bracing his administration for a storm of controversy which he felt would be at least as fierce as that surrounding his labour laws. His musing that any government agency or operation could be sold if selling it made sense was a turnabout from his predecessor's adamant "B.C. is not for sale." Said Vander Zalm:

> The privatization process is going to be a big thing and it's going to be daring. The mandate that I gave to the minister responsible was "Privatize."
>
> He said: "How much?"
>
> I said: "If you can give good reasons for the privatization of something we're presently involved with, look at it."
>
> "What about the parliament buildings?"
>
> "Fine. Privatize. But not the legislature."

Perhaps Bill Vander Zalm's greatest act of privatization, and over time the most controversial, was the privatization of the premiership. His highly personal leadership style blurred the accepted distinctions between the public and private life of a government leader. This is best exemplified by his continued association with his theme park, Fantasy Garden World. The premier and his wife live in a large second-floor apartment in their dream castle, where they are undoubtedly among the biggest attractions for tourists. Vander Zalm loves to retreat to his castle and his gardens every weekend to mingle with the people, spend time with his family and simultaneously conduct government business.

Critics suggest that the premier's promotion of his family business constitutes a conflict of interest, even though the business has been transferred to his wife. It has even been said that Vander Zalm gave up the finance portfolio after the election because the Canadian Imperial Bank of Commerce, Fantasy Garden World's chief creditor, also handles many provincial government accounts. Strictly speaking, the premier is not in violation of the conflict of interest guidelines he set in place shortly after the election. These guidelines, well intentioned but ambiguous, did not prevent ministers from quitting the cabinet over personal conflicts or improprieties.

Minister of Forests and Lands Jack Kempf was removed from the cabinet in March 1987 because of financial irregularities in the running of his office. (He was replaced by rookie Skeena MLA Dave Parker, the first professional forester ever to serve as a forest minister in British Columbia.) Also in March, Stephen Rogers, whose political career seemed perpetually plagued by controversies, was forced to step down as environment minister over allegations of conflict of interest. Vander Zalm shifted Rogers to the less compromising post of intergovernmental relations and also gave him responsibility for spearheading the government's privatization program. Then in July, Minister of Advanced Education Stan Hagen resigned his cabinet position when it was learned that he had failed to resign as president and director of his former business. Hagen was subsequently reinstated after an investigation by the deputy attorney general.

Although these affairs chipped away at the government's credibility, they also demonstrated Premier Vander Zalm's determination to deal quickly and efficiently with any hints, no matter how vague, of wrongdoing on the part of his cabinet. Vander Zalm had wanted to lead a squeaky-clean administration, different in style and make-up from the scandal-prone Bennett government. However, his first year in office only showed how difficult it was to get a handle on conflicts of interest and demonstrated the human failings and weaknesses inherent in any organization open to close and constant scrutiny. Indeed, many wondered if it was at all possible for successful individuals with business or professional experience to offer themselves for public service without someone, somewhere, crying conflict. The challenge remains to develop a system of financial disclosure or a conflict of interest code that will not discourage talented people from entering the political arena but will satisfy the public demand for ethical conduct.

Premier Vander Zalm's first year in office showed what kind of a leader he was, and it foretold a pattern for his government's behaviour. He had spent much of his time distancing himself from the previous Social Credit administration and attempting to prove his contention that style is substance. There was no question that his government had a different style and that there appeared to be some serious substance to the new directions being charted for the province. There remained, however, nagging doubts about the long-range plans of the Vander Zalm government and the premier's ability to manage the political reshaping of British Columbia, and fears that policy would eventually catch up to personality.

The inevitable comparisons were made with Bill Bennett, who now led a quiet semiretired life collecting the occasional board directorship. There were striking differences in style and approach, but there were also surprising similarities between the two which emphasized the universality of leadership. Bill Bennett had been an effective manager, steering the ship of state through treacherous, uncharted waters, making tough but necessary decisions to keep his ship afloat. At the same time, he was never revered as a leader, nor could he easily accept the adulation and praise that sometimes went with his job. Bill Vander Zalm, on the other hand, has strong leadership abilities and through his personal appeal has shown that his leadership style can win decisive political contests. Bill Bennett managed, but could not lead the province. Bill Vander Zalm has tremendous leadership potential, but can he manage?

In the leadership laboratory of British Columbia, only time will tell if Vander Zalm can meet the challenge and become a great premier. If he does not himself possess the natural ability to manage, he has the option of attracting the most loyal and competent elected and nonelected managers to help him do the job. Asked to identify his strengths and weaknesses as a leader, Vander Zalm said:

> My greatest strength is that I find it easy to get people to do things for me. And the people that I've worked with have always become totally committed. They've become very much a part of everything it is that I'm trying to do. I can get the right people around me, and I can get them to do the things that I want to see done, and they'll do them effectively. That's my strength.
>
> My weakness is that I'm very soft-hearted. I find that oftentimes if a decision is going to hurt someone, I may tend to put off the decision. I can work well with people, but I find it very difficult to do the Jimmy Pattison sort of thing, where if you're the low producer on the list, you're out. That type of strong approach I would find very difficult.

Bill Vander Zalm is uncomfortable with a growing tendency to compare him with his predecessor, but the fact remains that leadership has a dynamic of its own, universal traits which sometimes transcend changes of style and leaders. Vander Zalm as premier was often reacting to the actions of his predecessor, determined not to repeat Bennett's mistakes. But no leader is immune to the follies of history, and in the course of pursuing their own goals and objectives they can easily but perhaps unexpectedly discover themselves adopting the means of their predecessors to achieve new ends. David Poole said of Premier Vander Zalm's *modus operandi:* "The method of getting things done is probably identical to the method that Premier Bennett used. It's made more difficult by the fact that this premier wants it to look different. That's strong stuff, because I think a lot of people would be upset by it. But it's true."

The two premiers differ in their use of expert opinion, social research and polls. Bennett extensively used such data and was a master at interpreting polls, making a science of the art of politics. Vander Zalm, on the other hand, is a master of political intuition, relying almost exclusively on his gut feelings. Successful politicians have plenty of room to manoeuvre so long as they are within what John F. Kennedy referred to as "the jaws of consent." (Kennedy, who usually had confidence in his instincts, said the time to take a poll was when he had made a decision that might be "outside the jaws of consent.")

Bill Vander Zalm has the ability to become a great leader; and, like all leaders, he has the ability to self-destruct. With the honeymoon now fading, some may already forget his promise of reconciliation. He still holds that hope, but he must also come to grips with the perplexing problem of managing the provincial government, the largest business in British Columbia. He needs not only to manage it but to do so through a controversial period of restructuring. Therein lies Bill Vander Zalm's challenge, should he decide to accept it.

It is a special place that would embrace a leader such as Bill Vander Zalm and allow him to single-handedly set the tone of public discussion and set the pace of development heading towards the last decade of this century. British Columbia is still a frontier society characterized by extremes. Its rapid growth and development since the Second World War have shaped a dynamic political culture. The rise of British Columbia during W. A. C. Bennett's premiership compacted centuries of experience in industrialization into two rollicking decades of unbridled economic expansion. With this acceleration of the concentration and dispersion of wealth came a heightened sense of the ideological struggle between capitalism and socialism, individualism versus collectivism. This has manifested itself in the province's polarized politics, where the right wing has been further right and the left wing further left than elsewhere in Canada. Voices of moderation have in the recent past found only loneliness in a desperate search for a safe middle-of-the-road approach to B.C. politics. Those caught standing in the middle of the road have generally been run over.

In British Columbia it is the right-wing party that has best exemplified this radicalism. Earlier in the century it was the socialist parties, railing against the apparent inequities of the established order, who assumed the roles of social critics and advocates of reform. But the steady evolution and professionalization of socialist parties has seen them become not only respectable and accepted but also moderate and mainstream in their policy proposals.

In fact, the NDP has become the defender of the status quo in Canada, an integral part of the welfare state establishment. In British Columbia, the NDP is constitutionally aligned with the highly conservative forces of trade unionism and with a myriad of other pressure groups resisting change, and is increasingly supported by the white-collar class who can find no other comfortable political home in a radical environment.

The Social Credit Party, on the other hand, has been a consistent agent of radical change. Even though it has been the governing party for most of the past generation, it has continually challenged existing assumptions, struggled with the forces of the establishment and provided strong, often demagogic leadership. Many observers of B.C. politics and opponents of Social Credit have wrongly assumed that the party was a simple outgrowth of the old-guard Liberal and Conservative parties which dominated provincial politics for the first half of this century. This assumption is so patently wrong it is no wonder that the Socreds' opponents have for so long remained in opposition and B.C. politics has been so widely misinterpreted.

Social Credit was born as a party of protest. Its history shows that even protest parties can suffer the problems of staying in power for too long. The secret of political succession in a party such as Social Credit therefore becomes a unique challenge. Bill Bennett's brilliant but sad departure from public life set the stage for institutionalizing the Social Credit Party far beyond the leadership of the Bennett family. If Bill Vander Zalm is still premier of British Columbia in 1992, then his time in office, added to Bill Bennett's and Dave Barrett's, will together be equal to W. A. C. Bennett's record. And over a forty-year period, Social Credit will have been in power continuously, with only one three-year interruption. This would make the Social Credit Party of B.C. one of the most successful political institutions in Canadian history.

That one-term governments are the exception to the historical rule, combined with the tolerance of voters who usually want to give a government a second chance, could easily conspire to see Premier Vander Zalm serve a second term before thinking seriously about going "back to the garden." His leadership abilities will decide the fate of the populist party he leads. The political reshaping of British Columbia will meanwhile continue apace, changing the face of Canada's most blessed, most querulous province, and doing so against the resistance of established forces and entrenched interests.

The premier's greatest challenge will be to see if he can build a strong team to strengthen his government and to help broaden his party's appeal so that he can sustain his radical vision for reinvigorating and reindustrializing the province. Or can he do it alone?

And somewhere down the road, Premier Vander Zalm will also face the ultimate test of leadership: succession.

APPENDIX

The Top 20

From Marjorie Nichols's column "The Top 20: or, the B.C. Social Credit Party's Hit Parade," Vancouver *Sun*, 8 July 1986.

"Here is a list of the members, in alphabetical order:

"*Morris Belkin*, chairman of Belkin Inc.; *Sam Belzberg*, president of First City Trust; *Robert Bentall*, president of the Bentall group; *David Black*, of DuMoulin, Black, lawyers; *Peter Brown*, president of Canarim Investments; *Tom Buell*, president of Weldwood of Canada; *Robert Chilton*, Western Management; *J. V. Clyne*, retired B.C. Supreme Court justice; *Joseph Cohen*, vice-president of Sony of Canada; *Denis Cote*, chairman of the UMA Group Ltd.; *Bill Docksteader*, president of Bill Docksteader Motors Ltd.

"*Herb Doman*, president of Doman Industries; *Ian Falconer*, senior vice-president of Midland Doherty, stock and bond brokers; *Brian Fisher*, president of Jet Set Sam Services Inc.; *Brian Follet*, president of Hayhurst Communications; *David E. Gillanders*, of Lawson, Lundell, Lawson & McIntosh, lawyers; *Herb Goldman*, regional vice-president of Lavalin Inc.; *Donald W. Gordon*, Reed Stenhouse Limited, insurance; *D. Hank Gourlay*, president of Motrux Transportation Ltd.

"*Ronald Granholm*, president of The Johnston Group; *Abe Gray*, chairman of Gray Beverage Company; *Robert Hallbauer*, senior vice-president of Teck Corporation; *J. Grant Hammond*, Touche Ross and Company; *Brian L. Hauff*, president of INTREX; *Robert F. Hendy* (no listed occupation); *Tony Jarrett*, president of Fibreco Export Inc.; *Chester*

Johnson, chairman of B.C. Hydro; *Norm Kevil Jr.*, president of Teck Corporation.

"*John Kerr*, president of Lignum Sales Ltd.; *Robert Lee*, president of the Prospero Group; *Bill Levine*, president of Daon Corporation; *Bob Lunde*, Lomak Transport Corp., Prince George; *Gordon MacFarlane*, chairman of B.C. Telephone Co.; *G. W. MacLaren* (no listed occupation); *Patrick Mahoney*, McElhanney Group Ltd.; *Bev Machesney*, senior vice-president of McKim Advertising Ltd.; *J. R. (Dick) Maze*, senior vice-president of Lafarge Ltd.; *Bruce Nicoll*, vice-president of Canada Safeway Ltd.; *Les Peterson*, Boughton & Company; *Conrad Pinette*, president of Pinette & Therrien Mills, Williams Lake.

"*David Radler*, president of Sterling Newspapers Ltd.; *Fred W. Read*, president of Commonwealth Construction; *Terry Salman*, vice-president of Nesbitt Thomson Bongard Inc.; *Don C. Selman*, Wolridge, Mahon & Co.; *Ronald C. Shon*, president of The Shon Group; *Don Skagen*, chairman of Mohawk Oil Co. Ltd., Calgary; *Bill Sloan* (retired) of Sidney; *Ross Smith* of Peat Marwick Mitchell; *Fred Stimpson*, president of The Bills Group; *Gerry Strongman*, president of Tonecraft Realty Inc.; *Peter Thomas* of Lavacat Resources Ltd.

"*Steve Vrlak*, president of Vrlak, Robinson; *Al Wagner* of Northwest Pro-Tec-Tion Garments; *Michael P. Warren* of Owen, Bird; *Peter Webster* (no listed occupation); *John Whitmer*, president of Balfour Forest Products Inc., Prince George; *James A. Winton*, president of Block Bros. Industries Ltd.; *Fred Wu*, president of Triona Investments."

Note on Sources

The primary documentary sources for this book are the many political, government and business figures who have shared with me their observations, reflections and reminiscences about British Columbia's recent past. Because *Succession* represents an exercise in contemporary history, with most of the critical events still being played out on a stage where many of the actors continue to perform, it has obviously not been possible to consult with or interview all of the key players. I have necessarily been highly selective in my choice of whom I interviewed. Nevertheless, I attempted to concentrate on a cross-section of opinion leaders whose views on the recent succession of leadership in British Columbia's governing party would be both valuable and accessible.

The two most important interviews were with the two premiers who hold this book together. Both Bill Bennett and Bill Vander Zalm separately shared many hours of tape recorded recollections and opinions with me over the course of several sessions. Interviews with a select group of almost thirty other individuals were tape recorded between September 1986 and June 1987. Following is a complete list of the interviews conducted:

Michael Bailey
Bill Bennett
Michael Burns
Kim Campbell

John Laschinger
Graham Lea
Grace McCarthy
Bob McClelland

Hugh Curtis
Derek De Biasio
David Emerson
Garde Gardom
Charlie Giordano
Mike Harcourt
Peter Hyndman
Rita Johnston
Edgar Kaiser Jr.
Roberta Kelly
Patrick Kinsella
Jerry Lampert

Jim Nielsen
Jimmy Pattison
Don Phillips
John Plul
David Poole
Stephen Rogers
Bud Smith
Norman Spector
Peter Toigo
Bill Vander Zalm
Hope Wotherspoon

In addition to these "oral history" sources, I have relied upon and consulted the growing library of literature on B.C. history and politics as well as government documents and publications. *The Debates of the Legislative Assembly of British Columbia* (Hansard), *Budget Speeches, Journals* of the Legislative Assembly of British Columbia and *Statements of Votes*, Province of British Columbia, are among the indispensable reference materials for all students of B.C. government and politics.

Periodicals, magazines and newspapers which have reported upon or covered important aspects of politics in British Columbia during the years covered in this book include the *Canadian Annual Review*, the *Decima Quarterly Report, B.C. Studies, Maclean's, Western Report, Time, B.C. Business, Equity, The Financial Post*, the *Globe and Mail*, the Victoria *Times-Colonist*, the Vancouver *Province* and the Vancouver *Sun*.

The coverage of politics and government in British Columbia by the major urban daily newspapers is uneven and sometimes spastic but also influential, for the news media feeds, drives and even creates political issues. Future historians of British Columbia will be intrigued to review the work of the two premier political columnists of this era, both published in the Vancouver *Sun:* Marjorie Nichols and Vaughn Palmer. Their work often represents the polar extremes of opinion in the province and juxtaposes in entertaining fashion the policies, personalities and peculiarities of British Columbia public life. Nichols and Palmer went so far as to swear that they never read each other's columns—however, all B.C. politicians did, and most observers of politics also made their newspaper pieces part of a regular, unbalanced diet of crucial information and inflammatory opinion. Nichols, Palmer and other political columnists, such as the veteran Jim Hume of the Victoria *Times-Colonist*, as well as T.V. and radio journalists, played a major role in shaping the key issues and controversies of B.C. politics during the era covered in this book.

Following is a list of published secondary sources which proved valuable as background:

Allen, Robert C. and Gideon Rosenbluth, *Restraining the Economy: Social Credit Economic Policies for B.C. in the Eighties*. Vancouver: New Star, 1986

Anderson, Robert and Eleanor Wachtel, *The Expo Story*. Madeira Park, B.C.: Harbour Publishing, 1986

Blake, Donald E., R. K. Carty and Lynda Erickson, "Ratification or Repudiation: The Social Credit Leadership Convention." Paper delivered at the annual meeting of the Canadian Political Science Association, McMaster University, 6–8 June 1987

Blake, Donald E., *Two Political Worlds: Parties and Voting in British Columbia*. Vancouver: University of British Columbia Press, 1985

Boyle, T. Patrick, *Elections British Columbia*. Vancouver: Lions Gate Press, 1982

Carty, R. Kenneth and W. Peter Ward, *National Politics and Community in Canada*. Vancouver: University of British Columbia Press, 1986

Garr, Allen, *Tough Guy: Bill Bennett and the Taking of British Columbia*. Toronto: Key Porter, 1985

Magnusson, Warren et. al., *The New Reality: The Politics of Restraint in British Columbia*. Vancouver: New Star, 1984

Magnusson, Warren et. al., *After Bennett: A New Politics for British Columbia*. Vancouver: New Star, 1986

Martin, Patrick, Allan Gregg and George Perlin, *Contenders: The Tory Quest for Power*. Scarborough, Ontario: Prentice-Hall, 1983

Mitchell, David J., *W. A. C.: Bennett and the Rise of British Columbia*. Vancouver: Douglas & McIntyre, 1983

Mitchell, David J., "No Stopping Him—Change they wanted, and Bill Vander Zalm sure gave 'em that." *Vancouver*, October 1986

Morley, J. Terence et. al., *The Reins of Power: Governing British Columbia*. Vancouver: Douglas & McIntyre, 1983

Nichols, Marjorie and Bob Krieger, *Bill Bennett: The End*. Vancouver: Douglas & McIntyre, 1986

Ohashi, T. M. and T. P. Roth, *Privatization—Theory and Practice*. Vancouver: The Fraser Institute, 1980

Palmer, Bryan D., *Solidarity: The Rise and Fall of an Opposition in British Columbia*. Vancouver: New Star, 1987

Persky, Stan, *Son of Socred: Has Bill Bennett's government gotten B.C. moving again?* Vancouver: New Star, 1979

Persky, Stan, *Bennett II: The Decline and Stumbling of Social Credit Government in British Columbia 1979–83*. Vancouver: New Star, 1983

Twigg, Alan, *Vander Zalm: From Immigrant to Premier*. Madeira Park, B.C.: Harbour Publishing, 1986

Index

Printed in Canada